Daughters
of the
West

To Linda, from Charles
From the Pacific
Northwest
June 1999

*Other non-fiction books
by Anne Seagraves*

Soiled Doves: Prostitution In The Early West [©] 1994

High~Spirited Women Of The West [©] 1992

Women Who Charmed The West [©] 1991

Women Of The Sierra [©] 1990

Tahoe, Lake In The Sky [©] 1987

Beautiful Lake County [©] 1985

Daughters
of the
West

By Anne Seagraves

Copyright © 1996 by WESANNE PUBLICATIONS
Printed in the United States of America

Published by WESANNE PUBLICATIONS
Post Office Box 428
Hayden, Idaho 83835

Library of Congress Number 95-061859
ISBN 0-9619088-5-8

ACKNOWLEDGMENTS

COVER PHOTO:
Courtesy of the Collection of the National Cowgirl Museum
and Hall of Fame, Fort Worth, Texas

GRAPHIC DESIGNER: Sheila R. Bledsoe

Arizona Historical Society, Tucson, AZ; Arizona Pioneers' Historical Society, Tucson, AZ; Boise Public Library, Boise, ID; Boise State Historical Society, Boise, ID; Boise State University Special Collections Department, Boise, ID; Bonner County Historical Society Museum, Sandpoint, ID; Buffalo Bill Cody Historical Center, Cody, WY; California State Library, California Room, Sacramento, CA; Cheney Cowles Historical Museum, Spokane, WA; Coeur d'Alene Public Library, Coeur d'Alene, ID; Columbia State Park, Columbia, CA; Daughter's of the Republic of Texas Library, Austin, TX: Denver Public Library, Denver, CO; Eastern Washington Historical Society, Spokane, WA; El Dorado Historical Museum, Placerville, CA; Elmore Historical Society, Mountain Home, ID; Gila County Historical Archives, Globe, AZ; Hayden Public Library, Hayden, ID; Humbolt National Forest Service, Buhl, ID; Kelley House Museum, Mendocino, CA; Kings Ranch, Kingsville, TX; Idaho Historical Society, Boise, ID; Idaho Public Library, Boise, ID; Lake County Museum, Lakeport, CA; Lincoln County Historical Society, Davenport, WA; Mariposa Museum and History Center, Inc., Mariposa, CA; Mendocino Historical Research Inc., Ukiah, CA; Montana Historical Society, Helena, MT; National Cowgirl Hall of Fame Western Heritage Center, Fort Worth, TX; Nevada Historical Society, Reno, NV; Nevada State Library, Carson City, NV; North Idaho College, Coeur d'Alene, ID; Old Montana Prison, Deer Lodge, MT; Oregon Historical Society, Portland, OR; Pajaro Valley Historical Society, Watsonville, CA; Panhandle-Plains Historical Museum, Canyon, TX; Priest Lake Historical Society, Priest Lake, ID; Sierra City Historical Society, Sierra City, CA; Stanford University, Stanford, CA; Tabor Opera House, Leadville, CO; Texas State Historical Society, Austin, TX: United States House of Representatives, Washington, D. C.; Wells Fargo Bank Archives, San Francisco, CA; Wyoming State Museum, Cheyenne, WY and Yuma Territorial Prison State Historic Park, Yuma, AZ.

In researching Daughters of the West, many individuals have been extremely helpful. The author would like to thank the following people: Joan Benner, National Cowgirl Hall of Fame; Betsy Cammack, Sierra City Historical Society; Dorothy B. Crawford, Historian; Megan Coddington, Kelley House Museum; Ann Ferguson, Curator, Bonner County Historical Society Museum; Evelyn Furman, for permission to use photos from her private collection and brief quotes from her book, "The Tabor Opera House: A Captivating History;" Marion Geoble, Lake County Historian; Sherrin Grout, Columbia State Park; Alice Hicks and Patti McGrath of Mountain Home, Idaho, for making the story of Kittie Wilkins possible; Linda Offeney, Ranger/Curator, Yuma Territorial Prison State Historic Park: Muriel Powers, Historian, Mariposa Museum and History Center, Inc.; Bonnie Shields, Tennessee Mule Artist; Allan Virta, University Archivist, Boise State University.

AND A VERY SPECIAL THANK YOU TO:

Valle Novak, Sandpoint, ID, for professional editing; Sheila Bledsoe, Graphic Designer, Post Falls, ID, for outstanding artwork throughout the book, and as always, my husband, Wes, who has been with me every step of the way in writing this book.

FOREWORD

Between 1840 and 1870, the words "Wagons-Ho!" signaled the beginning of a mass migration that would forever change the face of America. Hundreds of thousands of men, women and children embarked upon a 2,000-mile journey across the continent in search of free land, gold, adventure and a better life. They traveled by wagon, horseback, pushcart or foot across an often inhospitable land, where danger lurked around every curve.

Although only a few women were numbered among the first pioneers, those who managed to survive the ordeal would never again be the same. The gentle wife, forced by her demanding husband to endure the dangers of the trail, found, to her own amazement, that she was stronger than she thought and often had more endurance than her mate.

When the journey was over, her husband was shocked to discover his docile wife had been replaced by a stronger woman, capable of handling almost any situation as well as she could her Winchester. She had been scorched by desert heat, crossed treacherous mountains and fought disease and Indian raids and did it successfully.

The Western women learned to handle a team, crack a whip and follow a plow. They expected to work beside their husbands as equal partners, for they had earned that right. As dutiful wives, they had also traded their comfortable homes in the East for what was supposed to be a charming house on the prairie, and found, instead, a half-finished log cabin, lean-to or dugout with earthen walls and a dirt floor. The ladies, however, made the best of the situation, for they had developed a respect for the land that gave them freedom as well as the courage to live in it.

That courage was often beyond belief. In 1868, in the Legion Valley of Texas, an act of terrible violence took place. Tiny, 18-year-old Matilda Friend, who was eight months pregnant, was attacked in her own home by a roving band of Indians. An arrow went through her side, another pierced her arm and a third struck her breast, then she was scalped. Little Matilda somehow managed to crawl, walk and drag her tortured body one and a half miles to receive help. Both the girl and her baby survived, but Matilda had to wear a cover over her head the rest of her life.[1]

[1]**Indian Depredations in Texas,** by J. W. Wilbarger, 1889

Another act of heroism occurred in 1867 when Mrs. Stevens, who lived on a ranch on the outskirts of Tombstone, Arizona, was left with only her hired hand while her husband drove into town. When a band of Indians attacked her cabin, Mrs. Stevens and her "hand" had a real shoot-out. A group of cowboys heard the shots and rode to their rescue. As the last Indian disappeared, a cowboy asked Mrs. Stevens if she wanted to send her husband a message. She grabbed her pen and scrawled, "Lewis, send me some more buckshot, I'm almost out."[1]

With so few women on the frontier, one young wife, after assessing the situation, remarked to a friend, "Guess my husband's going to look after me, and make himself agreeable to me, if he can. If he don't there's plenty will!" Another woman decided she didn't want anything to do with what she described as the broken-down, smelly, gun-toting men of the West, and returned home. Others struck out on their own to conquer and settle the harsh, new land.

These women were independent and ready to do things their own way. Mary Meager of Washington Territory became a successful rancher and cattlewoman. In California, Luzena Wilson opened what she called a "hotel." It consisted of two cots in a tent, but Luzena's business became so profitable that she made her husband her partner.

In Cascade, Montana, Mary Fields, a six-foot, 200 pound freed slave from Tennessee, began hauling freight. Mary became quite an expert with the team and was soon hired to drive the U.S. mail stage. She is reputed to have earned the dubious privilege of drinking with the men in the local saloons.

Miss Nellie Cashman, however, is considered to be one of the most independent and respected women of the mid-1800s. She was a no-nonsense girl from Ireland, who became part of the legend of the early West. Although Nellie was only five-feet tall and weighed less than 100 pounds, the Irish lass became America's first female prospector. Her many good deeds and heroism earned Nellie the title of "The Irish Angel of Mercy," and her life is an inspiration to women everywhere.

Whether they were wives, entrepreneurs or adventurers, these intrepid women became part of the West. They represented the feminine side of the American frontier and added a gentle touch to the otherwise uncivilized land.

---

[1]**Legendary Characters of Southeast Arizona,** by Ben. T. Traywick, 1992

Dedicated to:

The women who had the courage
to follow their dreams.

CONTENTS

---

*Cover Photo Courtesy of the Collection of the National
Cowgirl Museum and Hall of Fame, Fort Worth, Texas*

Valle Novak, Editor
Sheila R. Bledsoe, Graphic Designer

INTRODUCTION

The 19th century became an era of change for the American people. Social conditions in the eastern cities were becoming unbearable with overcrowding and unemployment. What was once a land of promise had become a narrow world with few opportunities, especially for women. The opening of the Western frontier offered hope for a new and better tomorrow and a mass migration began, which included a small percentage of women. Although most were married, a few desperate females attempted the trip alone. Those who lacked courage when they left soon acquired it out of necessity before the ordeal was over.

This action-packed book captures the feminine side of the West and tells of the colorful ladies who earned the respect of the male-dominated frontier. When these women first put their feet in the stirrups and looked at the world from the back of a horse, there was no holding them back — for they knew they were daughters of the West. Several of the more spirited women dared to reach out for the brass ring on the merry-go-round of life, and a few managed to catch it. Unfortunately, the historians seldom bothered to record their deeds.

In 1840, Sally Skull, a "spare" woman called "Mustang Jane," dressed in men's clothing and ruled the range with the six-shooters she wore on either side of her waist. She traveled the lonely territory in southern Texas known as "No Man's Land," wheeling and dealing in horses all the way. Sally became a heroine during the Civil War when she helped secure guns and ammunition for the Confederacy. Thirty years later, Kittie Wilkins, a beautiful golden haired woman known as "The Queen of Diamonds," rode sidesaddle beside her "hands," rounding up mustangs in Idaho, Nevada and Oregon. Kitty was a lady who lived by her own rules and the only woman of her era whose sole occupation was horse trading.

In Cheyenne, Wyoming in 1897, a spunky girl named Bertha Kaelpernick became the first cowgirl to compete against men in a male-dominated sport. Other daring cowgirls followed Bertha's lead and changed the world of rodeo. These dashing, memorable women rode to fame while adding life and more than a little spice to the dusty arenas.

In the 1850s, entertainers began traveling the kerosene footlight circuit, spreading their own special form of cheer to the lonely settlers. When the theaters and opera houses were built in the 1860s, eager audiences rushed to see the famous stars of the day. In 1879, when Tabor's Opera House opened in Leadville, Colorado, the beautiful Anna Held appeared in the famous Ziegfeld Follies — and the Westerners knew the bright lights of Broadway weren't far behind.

Following the early theater, Nell Shipman, a woman who dared to enter the male-dominated moving picture industry, produced her first silent film in 1922. Although Nell successfully brought the beauty of the northwest to the American screen, her story is one of adversity, tragedy and loss.

Many women of the 1800s for reasons of their own, discarded their dresses for male attire and lived their lives as men. Perhaps the saddest story to come out of the West is that of "Little Jo Monaghan," a society debutante who traded her life in the East for the lonely settlements of the frontier. Delia Haskett's life as a stage driver for Wells Fargo, however, was anything but sad. She drove the stage over the rugged trails of California from 1876 to 1885, and enjoyed every minute of it, fearing only the possibility of meeting up with Black Bart, the infamous bandit who terrorized the western stage-coach drivers.

The schoolmarms with a cause were a dominant force in the early West. They were strong, dedicated women who proved to the western male that the feminine touch was not necessarily a weak one. These dauntless ladies picked up their skirts, waded right in, and helped to educate the west as well as tame it.

Since success doesn't come to everyone, many women of the era made mistakes and broke the law. The petticoat prisoners were a sad lot who generally ended up in one of the uncomfortable cells of the territorial prisons. Pearl Hart, the most famous occupant of the Yuma Territorial Prison in Arizona, spent two years behind its bars. She was known as the last of the old-time stage robbers. Although it has been said that Pearl disappeared following her release, there are new records that show how the notorious lady spent the rest of her life.

These early-day women were a diverse group who belong to the magnificent Western frontier. Their vibrant, authentic stories portray a time that is gone forever and salute the spirit of those who had the courage to follow their dreams.

The stories of these remarkable women have been carefully researched and documented through the generous assistance of historians, librarians and the special collection departments of many leading universities.

I have spent years reading old, out-of-print books, biographies, newspapers dating from the mid-1800s to the mid-1900s, magazines, diaries, personal letters, public records, and correspondence.

As with all history, one must rely upon what others have written or recorded. In this book, I have attempted to create readable, accurate stories of the women of yesterday and their achievements.

— The Author

Courtesy of the Elmore Historical Society, Mountain Home, Idaho

Kittie Wilkins

"The Queen of Diamonds"

Chapter 1

HORSE TRADING LADIES AND CATTLE QUEENS

F rom the mid-1800s through the turn-of-the-century, women
with vision and business acumen were generally frowned upon
or ignored. It was a gun-toting male-dominated era, where
men like Wyatt Earp, Doc Holliday and Jesse James became famous.
As tales of their heroism and deeds spread throughout the land, historians reached for their pens and eagerly began to write about these
colorful characters who appeared to be the true heroes of the Wild
West.

Today, as researchers carefully delve into old records, documents and diaries, new names are coming forward — those of the
women. Historians are, at last, filling in the missing pages of time
with the wide-ranging feminine accomplishments of yesterday. Although long overdue, women of Western history are finally receiving the recognition they deserve.

In the 1870s, when a woman's place was in the home, a beautiful golden-haired woman was riding the range, sidesaddle, rounding
up wild mustangs. Her name was Kittie Wilkins, a lady who built an
empire that encompassed a large area of southern Idaho, northern
Nevada and eastern Oregon. In an era when women "just didn't do
that sort of thing," Kittie became an outstanding rancher and expert
dealer in horses and often was called "The Horse Queen of Idaho,"
or "The Queen of Diamonds," due to her diamond brand.

Kittie was born in 1857 in Jacksonville, Oregon. Her parents,
John R. and Laura Wilkins, were an ambitious couple who visited
many boomtowns of the west before settling in Challis, Idaho, where
they began raising cattle and horses. During her early years Kittie
lived in several western states. John and Laura, however, never ne-

glected their daughter's schooling. While her father taught her the horse trading business, Kittie's mother made sure she attended the finest schools. She grew into a well-educated woman who could ride the range, consummate a shrewd business deal, or sit at the piano to entertain guests.

Kittie always claimed she got her start as a small child when two of her father's friends each gave her a $20 gold piece to invest. When her father became involved in the stock company, he used the money to buy Kittie a filly, which started her in business. She soon acquired her own herd that numbered between 700 and 800 horses. Kittie was an expert horsewoman; it was said she could ride anything with four feet on the ground, or anything with one foot on the ground and three feet in the air.[1]

By the time she was 28, the Wilkins company had moved to the Bruneau Valley of Owyhee County, Idaho. Although the outfit consisted of Kittie's father and her three brothers, she was the undisputed head of the company. She claimed every unbranded mustang on their range, which ran from the Humbolt River in Nevada, to the Snake River in Idaho, and from Goose Creek County in Idaho to the Owyhee River in Oregon. Kittie had the hardest working outfit west of the Mississippi River. Her boys were riding almost constantly as the ranch broke and shipped 154 horses every two weeks. The Wilkins riders became known as the finest in the world.

Kittie rode the open range with her cowhands, roping and saddle-breaking. The newspapers described her as a striking, blue-eyed blonde who rode a palomino the color of her hair. Seated upon a saddle that was mounted in silver and gold, Kittie was one with her horse as he flew over the rough terrain, rounding strays into the holding corrals.

When traveling to the Eastern stockyards, Kittie took two trunks, one for her work-clothes and the other for her fancy outfits, which were worn with a flair. Although she raised more than one eyebrow, the talented lady personally watched over her own horses, disdaining the idea that women were limited to playing the piano and attending tea parties. The herd was more important to her than the whispered gossip of others.

Because she was totally feminine, Miss Wilkins never failed to create excitement as she entered the marketplace. While selling her horses, the lady pulled her golden hair up under a hat and dressed in skillfully tailored mannish attire, something that was unheard of in

[1] **Idaho Women in History**, by Betty Penson-Ward, 1991

that era. Whatever her attire, however, Kittie knew her business. She found a way to move the abundant wild mustangs of the West to the horse-hungry markets of the East.

One time, she brought 3,000 head with her to St. Louis, Missouri, and auctioned them off herself, turning a tidy profit. It was rumored that the beautiful woman could make a better deal than her male counterparts and, in 1891, Kittie Wilkins was the only female in the United States whose sole occupation was horse dealing.

Once the horse trading was over, Kittie changed her male attire and met the press wearing the most stylish fashions. In 1895, during an interview, a reporter told his friends he was hardly prepared to meet the tall young woman "dressed in a svelte, tailor-made costume, her blond curls surmounted by a dainty Parisian creation, who greeted him with perfect self-possession and invited him to be seated."[1] He said she was a strikingly handsome woman. In 1904, at the age of 46, Kittie visited San Francisco. During her stay, she was a guest of the city and awarded "The Palm for Beauty," which meant she was the toast-of-the-town.

Often a cowboy who rode over the large Wilkins spread looking for a job, was surprised to find that "Kit" Wilkins was a she, not a he. At first, many of the men weren't sure they wanted to work for a female. However, once they realized the beautiful lady could not only handle her horse, but would also ride beside them, they always hired on. All of her "boys" were paid $40 a month and board, and they were strong, rough riders. Kittie ruled with an iron hand. If a cowboy got out of line, he was immediately fired. In a magazine article, one of her "hands" wrote: "If a man weren't a good rider when he went to work for Kit Wilkins, he was a good rider when he left or he wasn't riding at all — unless in a hearse."[2]

Many of Kittie's riders hired on as apprentices, and, under her guidance, became excellent cowboys. A few of them went on to fame in the Wild West Shows and others performed in rodeos. Hugh Strickland became a Champion of the World several times, Jess Coates rode before the King and Queen of England in a Command Performance, and Walter Scott became part of Buffalo Bill Cody's show, then became known as Death Valley Scotty.

Kittie was kind to her crew and earned their admiration as a skilled rider. She was not afraid of the unbroken horses and would enter the pens and manage the most unruly. She knew more about pedigrees than most women did about stylish clothes. With all her

[1]**St. Louis Post**, 1895
[2]**True West**, July-August, 1964

wealth and beauty, however, Kittie never married. It had been rumored she loved only one man. He was her top foreman and superintendent, and they were reportedly engaged to be married. Unfortunately, he was killed while trying to remove an intruder from the Wilkins spread and Kittie was true to his memory the rest of her life.

Kit raised her horses on "Wilkins Island," a high plateau between what was then called "Kittie's Hot Hole" and the mining area of Jarbidge, Nevada. The Hot Hole was a natural hot springs at the bottom of a gorge, and today is known as "Murphy's Hot Springs." The island was the company's headquarters where Kittie's "hands" built a corral that held the horses until they were shipped on to the eastern markets.

As Kittie rode the range and worked beside her cowboys, they shared a special camaraderie. Often, after a hard weeks work, she and her hands would ride into town and visit the local tavern for a bit of rest and frivolity. On one of these occasions, the Wilkins' boys were so carried away with their fun-making that someone "accidentally" opened the corral gate and the entire herd of captured "dollars" escaped.

Mrs. Alice Hicks, of Mountain Home, Idaho, remembers both Kittie and the tavern, as her father, Elijah Fletcher, once worked for the Wilkins. In a letter, she described a day in which she and her brother rode into town with their father to buy beef. Kit was standing in the door of the tavern and she greeted Elijah in a friendly manner saying, "Hello Lige, come on in and join the boys." When her father left the children sitting in the wagon, Mrs. Hicks recalls being a bit upset because at that young age she considered a tavern a den of "sin".

Although respectable women of that period didn't enter a tavern, it must be remembered that Kittie Wilkins was not an ordinary woman. She was always a lady, but she lived by her own rules.

Kittie had a lively personality and was a polished publicist. Her news releases were consistent and timely. She never deviated from her original tale of how she got her start with the two $20 gold pieces. Kittie's beauty and her success stories made headlines from San Francisco to St. Louis. Reporters admired her and the public enjoyed reading about the charming woman who many called "The Golden Queen." On December 17, 1927, *The Idaho Statesman* carried the following story, which was written in 1887, when Kittie was 30 years old. "Miss Wilkins, the 'Horse Queen of Idaho,' is at the Palace

Hotel. She arrived direct from her residence on the Bruneau River in Owyhee County. Miss Wilkins is one of the most noted women of the West. She early engaged in the stock business and has amassed a fortune."

Kit also was a unique woman who cared about the welfare of her cowboys. When a young 17 year old man, Harvey St. John, hired on as an apprentice, he became her friend. She encouraged him to get an education because, as she put it, "My boy, you will be here many years after the last mustang has trotted up the last chute."[1] Later in life, when St. John spent his holidays with her, she always greeted him with, "How is my youngest bronc rider?"

Her generosity extended beyond the welfare of the cowboys who rode beside her on the ranch. Kittie supported an orphanage in Salt Lake City, Utah, and she donated to a Catholic academy near San Francisco. When the boys were old enough to work, they were hired as hands for the Wilkins company. Several of the girls were taken into Kittie's home to assist with the housework, and a few she sent on to further their education. Numerous letters of appreciation from those who Kittie helped are on file, along with her property deeds and old records. One of the letters was from a mother requesting Kittie to take her boy to the west where he would be away from the crimes of the eastern city. Miss Wilkins was known and respected everywhere she went.

No matter how kind and generous a person is, there are always a few who find fault. Kittie's non-traditional lifestyle left her open to criticism. When a young teacher remarked how nice it was of Miss Wilkins to donate money to an orphanage, another lady responded, "Well, she should take care of those children because some of them are probably hers!" However, there was never a rumor of Kittie being involved in any scandal. She lived an open, honest life.

As time passed and Kittie grew older, she may have tinted her hair a bit, but she never lost that inner spark that made her so special. She rode over the range on her high-stepping horse a free woman who had a great love for animals and humanity. When she died of a heart attack in 1935, at the age of 79, no one thought of Kittie as an old woman. Although Miss Wilkins was one of the best known women of her generation, there has been very little written about her. Bits and pieces of Kittie's colorful life have come from old newspaper articles, a few paragraphs here and there, and through the courtesy of the Elmore Historical Society in Mountain Home, Idaho. It would

[1]**True West,** July-August, 1964

appear that one almost had to be notorious in order to become famous!

Long before Kittie Wilkins was born, another woman was actively engaged in the trading of horses. Her name was Sally Skull, a legendary woman from Texas, who wore a gun on either hip and was not afraid of the devil himself.

Sally has been described as a "spare woman" with sun-burned blonde hair and fiery blue eyes. She dressed in men's clothing and was known as "Juana Mesteña," or "Mustang Jane," on both sides of the Rio Grande River. Sally did not ride sidesaddle, as was the custom for women of that period. She would leap astride her Spanish pony, Redbuck, and take off at a gallop with her Mexican cowboys, the vaqueros, by her side. Together, they rode the unfenced range in an area called "No Man's Land," near Banquette, Texas.

Although Sally Skull is recognized for aiding the Confederacy during the Civil War, it is hard to draw a line between fact and fiction when chronicling her life. Sally, like Belle Starr and Calamity Jane, appears to be a strong woman who was born before her time.

She has been described both as a merciless killer, when aroused, as well as a woman of great compassion. Colonel Henry Perkins, in his Texas histories, wrote that Sally was a person who won his sincere friendship and admiration because of her devotion to others and many acts of kindness.[1] In the eyes of the Colonel, she was a lady of honor and spirit. Yet, another Texas gentleman said his mother used to threaten the children with, "Be good or old Sally Skull will get you!" Whatever the true story, Sally Skull was as colorful a character as Billy the Kid, and as such, she deserves to be remembered.

Sally's early years are obscure, It is believed she was the youngest of 13 children, born around 1820. Her parents were respectable people who moved from Philadelphia to Texas, when Sally was a child. The girl adapted easily to the wild, untamed lifestyle of the Texas frontier. So easily, that she ran off with her first husband while in her early teens. After that brief encounter, she married a man named Robertson and divorced him to become the wife of George Skull. Two children later, she again became a scandalous divorcee with a boy and girl to raise. Her husband kept his son and Sally placed her daughter in a good boarding school.

With her past behind, Sally became a daring horse trader, traveling across the Mexican boarder from the Texas frontier, wheeling and dealing all the way. She bought her horses in Mexico, put her

[1]**Frontier Times,** November, 1928

Circle S brand upon them, and drove the herd back to the States to sell for a profit. She never knew where the horses came from or cared.

Although the range was filled with dangerous renegades and desperadoes, they were probably more afraid of Sally Skull than she was of them. It was said she would kill any man she felt deserved to die and that she had a vocabulary that would cause a hardened criminal to cringe.

Sally became known as Mustang Jane, a woman who rode with a rifle in front of her saddle and pistols on either side of her waist. Jane could shoot with both hands and she was a crack shot. Her skill with the whip was so accurate that a twist of her wrist would sever a rosebud from its branch or a cigarette from the lips of a man. She never looked for trouble, but anyone who crossed her knew what the consequences would be.

Due to her daring and skill, Sally became a wagon boss during the Civil War. She took large wagon trains loaded with cotton over primitive roads from east Texas to Brownsville, and on to the Gulf to be loaded on English ships. As the war progressed, Sally was responsible for hauling hundreds of bales of cotton and trading them for the much needed ammunition and supplies which she brought back to the Confederacy. Although the journey was slow and dangerous, and the territory swarmed with ruffians, Sally always completed her mission. She rode into peril beside the vaqueros who were loyal to the lady they fondly called Juana Mesteña.

Sally carried a large money belt around her waist. She preferred to deal in cash and was respected for her honesty. The countryside was overrun with bandits and robberies were frequent, however, these desperate men left Sally alone. It was said they were afraid of her blazing guns, but perhaps it was because under their hard skins these renegades had a grudging respect for the lady herself.

There wasn't much in the way of entertainment for a woman like Sally. She didn't fit in with the men and stayed as far away from the ladies as possible. Two things she did enjoy were dancing and gambling. Many evenings she and her vaqueros would ride across the border into Mexico to dance until dawn. In Mexico, Juana Mesteña was a welcome sight as she spoke Spanish fluently and admired the people. One story tells of Juana dancing the fandango and of a stranger who dared to make insulting remarks. The next day, she found the man, pulled her guns from their holsters and peppered the ground at his feet. The sorry stranger performed a jig of his own until she put the pistols away. The lady obviously did not take criticism lightly.

On occasion, Sally would put a colorful blanket on Redbuck, polish his fine Spanish saddle, and ride to one of the gambling houses at Old St. Mary's or Matamoros, Mexico. These were popular haunts of the many famous gamblers Sally often played with in a win-or-lose session. In these places, she was respected as a gambler who could hold her own at the tables and always played a hard, honest game.

All of Sally's ventures were not successful, however. She was known as a marrying woman, and one day she finally married the wrong man, a Mr. Horsdorff. Colonel Perkins recalls seeing Sally Skull leave with her husband, and a large sum of money around her waist, on an excursion to buy horses. Her husband returned alone and Sally was never seen again.

Today, the colorful woman known as Mustang Jane, Juana Mesteña and Sally Skull is remembered as a lady of character and courage. In 1971, a Confederate Memorial Marker to honor Sally Skull was erected in Refugio County, Texas, at the intersection of Highway 202 and 182. The lady is gone but definitely not forgotten.

Horse trading ladies were not the only queens of the West. There are a few women's names sprinkled here and there among the hundreds of cattle kings and barons. Unfortunately, most of these ladies followed their husbands over the dusty trails to either an early grave or obscurity.

Lizzie Johnson, however, was not the following kind. At the age of 28, this robust woman registered her own brand, donned a sunbonnet and set out to become one of the first cattle queens in the state of Texas. Although Lizzie was female and married late in life, she went on to amass a fortune and became known as "Queen of the Trail Drivers."

Elizabeth (Lizzie) Johnson was born in Missouri in 1843, the second of six children. Her father, Thomas Jefferson Johnson, a professor, moved with his wife Catherine, and their children, to Hays County, Texas, where he established the Johnson Institute. The institute was the first school of higher learning west of the Colorado River in Texas. It was known for providing a fine education combined with a lot of discipline. Professor Johnson was a religious man who vigorously opposed the use of alcohol, and he passed his beliefs on to the students.

Lizzie was educated at the institute and grew into a severe young woman with a strong moral character. At the age of 16, she started teaching in her father's school, and eventually became so proficient at bookkeeping, that she began keeping books for many wealthy cattlemen. Lizzie also excelled at journalism and added to her income by writing for newspapers and magazines. She kept the extra money a secret from her family, investing it in cattle.

The Civil War had been a boon to the cattle business. During those bitter war years, while the men were in the army, cows strayed wherever they pleased over the unfenced range. Soon thousands of unclaimed calves roamed the land, providing an increase in unbranded herds that caused the value of Texas beef to drop. The maverick cattle were free for the taking, and Lizzie, always an opportunist, took advantage of the situation to expand her bank account.

In 1871, she registered her own brand in the county record book and joined the hundreds of men who were combing the hills for strays. Lizzie hired cowboys to help her round up the unbranded cattle and shipped the herds north where mature beef was in demand. In this manner, she added considerably to her holdings, becoming a very wealthy woman.

Eight years later, at the age of 36, Lizzie fell in love with Hezekiah Williams, an eligible widower with several children. No doubt Hezekiah was her first love, as she had a reputation for being a moral woman. When the handsome gentleman requested her hand in marriage, the lady was overcome with happiness. Their wedding ceremony was elaborate with Lizzie dressed to the nines in a bell-shaped skirt with a voluminous train. Although she was older than the average bride of that era, no young woman could have been more radiant.

Lizzie had good reason to be happy. She not only captured the heart of a handsome man, she also coerced him into signing a contract stating that her property, along with all future gains made by her, belonged to her. Lizzie was definitely a woman who was not lead by her heart. She always looked out for her own interests.

The contract proved to be a blessing, however, as Hezekiah turned out to be a poor businessman and Lizzie was constantly bailing him out of bad investments. She carefully watched over her husband's ventures and was recognized as the power behind him. When she found out Hezekiah was also a drinking man, Lizzie was quite upset. She said that religion and alcohol didn't mix, so Hezekiah never drank while in the company of his wife. He was an easy going man who wanted to keep peace in the family. Although Lizzie claimed to be a religious woman, this did not keep her from making what some would consider a shady deal!

In 1881, ten years after Lizzie recorded her brand, Hezekiah began trading cattle under a separate brand. They each ran their own business. Lizzie was always the one who never came out on the losing end of any situation.

During 1886 and 1889, Lizzie and Hezekiah traveled the Chisholm Trail as two independents. Lizzie was the first woman to drive her own herd with her own brand over the trail that stretched from San Antonio, Texas, to Abilene, Kansas. The hazardous trip was considered to be for only the strongest and most courageous men. But Lizzie, who loved her silks and satins, happily traded them for cotton dresses and a bonnet and hitched up her buggy.

Riding behind her herd, this strong, healthy woman proved she was a match for any man. She ate sow-belly and "pone" bread without complaint and crossed hundreds of miles of dangerous Indian country. At the end of the journey, Hezekiah and Lizzie sold their cattle to the highest bidder. It was rumored that Lizzie made the best deal without help from any male, and she became known as the "Queen of the Trail Drivers." Lizzie and Hezekiah made the trip over the old trail many times before it was abandoned in 1889.

After her trips up the trail, Lizzie became a unique breed of woman. She preferred the company of men and loved the cattle business, yet retained her feminine qualities. While on the trail or in the market trading cattle, Lizzie was accepted among the men as an equal. In private life, she wore luxurious gowns of the latest fashion. Her diamonds, valued at about $10,000, were admired by all and the envy of many. She expected, and received the courtesies of a refined lady.

Lizzie and Hezekiah traveled constantly and were recognized in the largest cities. Lizzie had a way of letting people believe they would get her business, or a sizable donation, if they treated her right. She always received the finest rooms, the best service and gourmet meals, but she never parted with a penny. In this manner, she kept everyone at her beck and call, anticipating a bit of her money they never received. She did not have a pleasant personality, so Lizzie used her wealth to gain popularity.

Hezekiah's health began to fail, and in 1914, when Lizzie was 71, he died. She was devastated and sadly brought her husband back to Austin, Texas, to be buried. "She paid $600 for his casket, no small amount in those days, and it is said she wrote a cryptic message across the bill which she returned to the undertaker, 'I loved this old buzzard this much.'"[1]

Following Hezekiah's death, Lizzie was at loose ends. She retained her business interests, which continued to thrive, but she was unhappy. Lizzie ceased to care about her appearance and within a few years, she resembled a pauper. Her shabby clothing made people pity her and even give money, thinking she was needy. Although Lizzie was very wealthy, she always kept the money for she had become a miser. Her barren room was cold and her food sparse, but her money continue to grow.

In 1923, Lizzie moved in with her niece. She was 80 years old and an eccentric who wandered about talking to herself. A year later, Lizzie died at the age of 81. When her family went through her belongings, they found money hidden in forgotten places, locked boxes containing parrot feathers beside flowers from Hezekiah's funeral, and her precious jewelry wrapped carelessly in a scorched cloth. Needless to say, she left a vast amount in business interests and assorted bank accounts.

Lizzie was buried next to Hezekiah in Austin, Texas. She was a strong, Texas woman who is admired for her business acumen as well as her ability to ride the rough trails beside the cattlemen of the West.

Unlike Lizzie Johnson, Henrietta King was not a cattle queen, she was queen of the King Ranch in Kingsville, Texas, and a woman of great strength and courage.

When her husband, Captain Richard King died in 1885, Henrietta inherited a half-million acres of land and a half-million dollar debt. She had always been a partner to her husband of 31 years. Together, they had enlarged their holdings from a small shelter to an elegant mansion, while raising five children.

Henrietta was a strong woman who had lived through many violent chapters of Texas history. With her husband gone, she was not about to give up in despair. Determined to keep what she had helped to build, Henrietta rolled up her sleeves and vigorously went to work.

With the aid of her son-in-law, she abandoned the old cattle drives in favor of modern transportation. Henrietta found new ways to bring water to the parched land and began raising ranch horses instead of workhorses. She eventually started a new breed of beef

[1]**Lizzie E. Johnson: A Cattle Queen of Texas**, by Emily Jones Shelton,
The Southwestern Historical Quarterly Vol. 2, Jan., 1947 no. 3

cattle, the Santa Gertrudis, for which the King Ranch is famous throughout the world.

The town of Kingsville, as well as many enterprises, were developed because of her hard work and determination. When Henrietta passed away in 1925, at the age of 93, she left an estate valued at $5.4 million and over a million acres of land, making the King Ranch one of the largest in the world.

Henrietta King is a fine example of what a Western woman could do when she made up her mind to turn a disaster into an outstanding success.

Although the horse trading women and cattle queens added excitement and color to the early west, there was also a need for the quieter, "mothering women." Both Elizabeth Boyle Smith and Mary Ann Goodnight were warm, nurturing ladies who were busy with their own families, but took time to care for the needs of others.

Elizabeth Boyle was born in Scotland in 1848. She was a well-educated, large woman with a twinkle in her eyes and a love of adventure. When her four brothers left Scotland to settle in America, Elizabeth packed her bags and followed, claiming they needed someone to "keep house."

Her new home was Fort Griffin, Texas, said to be one of the wildest towns in the west. Saloons, gambling houses and brothels lined Main Street and a shooting a day was not uncommon. However, the Scottish lass, who was raised in a strict Presbyterian home, didn't bat an eye. She took it in stride and accepted the town as it was.

Her arrival coincided with Fort Griffin's annual New Year's Ball. It was the season for the social event of the year that drew people from all over the area. Elizabeth was one of the oldest unmarried women in Fort Griffin and very shy. She had no desire to attend the affair, but finally gave in to her brothers' pleas. With her hair carefully curled and fluffed, Elizabeth put on her finest gown and set forth to join in the festivities, unaware that she would meet "Hank" Smith, a man who would change her life.

Hank was one of the many legendary males of Texas. He was admired for his bravery in the battlefield and respected as an honest businessman. Like Elizabeth, Hank was a quiet person. He could tell a good story, when called upon, but preferred to sit and smoke his pipe in solitude while watching the activities around him. Though many women had set their caps for him, Hank at 38, was still unattached. When Elizabeth arrived at the Ball, he knew she was the woman he had been waiting for.

Elizabeth and Hank were married a few months later, and became the owners of the town's Occidental Hotel. With a home of her own, the new Mrs. Smith planted flowers, hung lace curtains at the windows and put her beautiful china in a fine cabinet to be admired. The old hotel soon became the most popular place for miles around. Elizabeth had created comfort and hospitality in an otherwise rough town.

While Hank ran his wagon yard and livery stable, his wife, who was affectionately called "Aunt Hank," cooked wonderful meals. She never turned anyone away hungry, and a cowboy, who was down on his luck, could count on a good dinner and a bed for the evening at Aunt Hank's. Elizabeth felt all people were equal and welcomed the desperadoes as well as the men wearing a badge. Stovepipe Joe, Snakey Jim and Brazos Bill all enjoyed her generosity, as long as they did not create trouble. In return, these men watched over Elizabeth when Hank was away on business.

In 1877, Hank acquired a ranch in Bianco Canyon, a remote area of southern Texas. He built Elizabeth a big rock house where they raised their five children. The new home was 160 miles from civilization, but that didn't prevent Elizabeth from welcoming everyone who appeared at her door. Her first guests were curious Indians, followed by lonely buffalo hunters, weary travelers and adventurers. Doc Holliday was one of the famous guests who enjoyed Elizabeth's hospitality. It was said Doc needed at least two or three quarts of Red Eye daily to keep going, but he never appeared to be intoxicated. Doc wouldn't have dared to do so, for Elizabeth allowed no drunkenness in her home, and the men respected her wishes.

The Rock House became a haven for the ill and injured. Due to the isolation of the area, Aunt Hank kept a special room ready, with an extra supply of medicines. It was said she nursed everything from gun shot wounds to pneumonia. This remarkable woman had the energy and created the time to tackle almost anything. The Rock House became a place for social gatherings, the site of the first schoolhouse and a post office, with Aunt Hank as Postmistress.

Hank died in 1912, and Elizabeth remained in the home he had built for her many years before. She continued her life, helping others and mothering all who needed comfort. When Aunt Hank passed away at the age of 77, she had lived in the Rock House for 47 years.

Elizabeth "Aunt Hank" Boyle Smith is remembered as a benevolent woman who did all she could to ease the suffering and loneliness of the frontier. She lived with dignity and is known as "Mother of the West Texas Plains." In 1988, Elizabeth became a Western Heritage Honoree in the National Cowgirl Hall of Fame.

Eleven years before Elizabeth was born, Mary Ann Dyer entered the world in Madison County, Tennessee. She was the adored daughter of Susan and Joel Henry Dyer, a prominent lawyer, and the only girl among a large family of boys. Mary Ann grew up with the amenities of the city in the comfort of a fine home. At the age of 30, she met and married Colonel Charles Goodnight, and traded her life of ease for the loneliness of the Palo Duro Canyon of Texas. The nearest neighbor was 200 miles away.

Mary was a slight, gentle woman who was an accomplished horsewoman but not accustomed to driving a team. Being married to Charles Goodnight, however, meant she would participate in almost all forms of ranch life. Mary learned to patch cowboy's clothing and attended the ill and injured. Her life was so solitary that when a cowboy rode in with three chickens in a sack, she considered it a blessing. Mary claimed they were someone to talk to and wrote in her diary, " . . . they would run to me when I called them, and followed me every where I went. They knew me and tried to talk to me in their language."[1]

Mary began teaching Sunday school and conducted church services. Often, the lonely cowboys would ride long distances to spend that special day with her. They would remove their hats, slick down their hair and bow their heads in prayer. It wasn't the denomination that counted, it was the silent communication and the sharing of their love and respect for the Lord.

Mary and Charles Goodnight always welcomed weary travelers. Mary would see them first, as they approached miles away, and she would run to the kitchen to put on a huge pot of coffee and prepare a warm meal. Like Elizabeth Smith, Mary Ann brought cheer to the desolate plains.

When the slaughter of the buffalo almost brought them to extinction, Mary set aside 150 acres of the Goodnight Ranch. The acres were sown with wheat and became a haven for the large beasts of the plains.

During her lifetime, Mary Ann was a friend to all. She was kind to the Indian women as well as the white ladies, and is credited with

[1]**Charles Goodnight: Cowman and Plainsman**, by J. Evetts Haley

building churches, a college and a hospital. When she died in 1926 at the age of 87, Mary Ann Goodnight was recognized as the "Little Mother of the Texas Panhandle."

The horse trading ladies, cattle queens and mothering women were all part of the female influence upon the West. Together, they helped carve a civilization out of a wilderness while adding comfort and more than a bit of spice to the American frontier.

Miss Kittie Wilkins

She was a lady who lived by her own rules.

Kittie Wilkins "Horse Queen"
Died Suddenly

". . .'Diamond Field' Jack Davis was once an employe (sic) of Miss Wilkins. Davis was in 1897 convicted of the murder of two sheepmen . . . He was sentenced in Cassia county court to be hanged. The sentence was commuted at the last minute by the board of pardons to a life sentence in the state prison.

Miss Wilkins was born in Jacksonville, Ore., in 1857. As a girl she came to Boise with her family and lived in a home on the corner now occupied by the Hotel Boise. In the early 1890's, Miss Wilkins moved to Bruneau and began the horse business in which she was engaged until a few years ago.

In 1934 she was an honor guest at the Boise Centennial exhibition, riding a horse-drawn carriage in the pioneer parade.

It was her herd of more than 4000 horses that earned Miss Wilkins the title of 'horse queen' by which she was known, not only in the west but in eastern stock markets. She sold hundreds at a time. In one deal she is reputed to have disposed of 500 animals. The United States cavalry was a steady customer.

On a trip to Omaha while the business was in its prime, a pioneer friend recalled Miss Wilkins found there was no market for horses by the head so she sold her string by the pound.

The Owyhee mountains and the head of the Bruneau river was (sic) range for her stock. In addition to Wilkins Island — the home ranch which was not on an island but on land at the fork of the Bruneau near Jarbidge mountain — the family maintained winter camp, and several branches along the Snake. The Wilkins company also had holdings at Tuscaroro, Nev., where Miss Wilkins lived before coming to the Bruneau.

Some acquaintances of the horse queen maintain that Diamond Field Jack Davis was a ranch hand for several years of the neighboring Harvey family, however, and frequented the Wilkins range and ranches.

— Excerpts from the *Idaho Statesman*, October 9, 1936

Sally Skull

A horse trading lady

Confederate Memorial Marker

There is a Confederate Memorial marker in Refugio County, Texas, at the intersection of State Highway 202 and U.S. 182 near the location of Sally Skull's main ranch at Blanconia, (also known as Pull Tight and Dark Corner) which reads:

"Sally Skull was a woman rancher, horsetrader, 'champion cusser.' She ranched northwest of Refugio. In the Civil War she drove freight wagons with cotton from Texas to Mexico to swap for guns, ammunition, medicine, coffee, shoes, clothing and other goods vital to the Confederacy.

Dressed in trousers, Mrs. Skull bossed armed employees. She was a sure shot with the rifle she carried on her saddle or the two pistols strapped to her waist."

The spelling was casual, often phonetic, in the days of Sally Skull. This resulted in her name also appearing as Skull and Skulle. Her real name was Sarah Jane Newman, (or Nueman), Robinson Skull Doyle Wadkins Horsdorff. She adopted the alias of the one man she really loved and was known by that name most of her life.

— Courtesy of Dorothy F. Crawford, taken from her notes from the Daughters of the Republic of Texas.

Elizabeth Boyle Smith and family

Elizabeth was affectionately called "Aunt Hank."

Courtesy of the Panhandle-Plains Historical Museum, Canyon, Texas

Mary Ann Goodnight
She was known as "The Little Mother of the Texas Panhandle."

The Cowgirls

Kitty Canutt, Prairie Rose Henderson and Ruth Roach

Chapter 2

RODEO TRAIL

The first cowgirls were rugged daughters of the frontier who were cradled in the saddle and cut their teeth on a leather harness. Most of them learned to ride out of necessity as they helped on the ranch and practiced the skills of the range. At an early age, they could stay in the saddle, break a bronc and rope a steer. During the late 1800s, the younger horsewomen began competing against males in a yearly gathering of the herds, and from there, it was just one short step to participating in the rodeos.

The first rodeos began in the mid-1800s when thousands of cattle and horses were driven to town for the yearly round-up. The cowboys, eager for relaxation and fun, would compete in tests of skill, roping, breaking horses, branding cattle and racing. These round-ups became an important part of frontier life and developed into a celebration that usually occurred around the Fourth of July. They were often called Stampedes or Pioneer Days, and people came from miles around to participate in the festivities. These celebrations grew into rodeos and Wild West Shows.

Although a few daring women had participated in the early round-ups, they were not recognized in the arena until 1885, when Buffalo Bill Cody added a tiny sharpshooter named Annie Oakley to his Wild West Show. Annie, whose real name was Phoebe Ann Moses, knew nothing about horses, but she was an expert markswoman who skyrocketed to fame as "Little Sure Shot."

Within a few years, many talented horsewomen became a part of the Wild West shows; none, however, came close to Annie Oakley in fame. Miss Oakley was one of America's most distinguished entertainers. Wearing a broad-brimmed hat, and a fringed skirt which reached her knees, at a time when an exposed ankle was considered scandalous, she represented the romance of the Early West. Annie was part of a "man's world," yet her modesty and femininity commanded the respect of all who knew her. During her lifetime, the petite performer broke records with her shooting skills, appeared before the royal families of Europe and captured the heart of the world.

Although female performers had been accepted in the Wild West shows, it took a little longer before a woman dared to enter rodeos. In 1897, Bertha Kaelpernick rode over 100 miles to enter a horse race in Cheyenne's Frontier Days, and she was allowed to enter only because the arena was so muddy the cowboys refused to participate. Bertha was coerced into riding a bucking horse to keep the crowd from leaving. Once upon the animal, the petite girl had the ride of her life. Part of the time the horse was up in the air on his hind feet and once he fell backwards, but gutsy Bertha skillfully slid to his side and hung on. Although it was said at that time, that Bertha was a terrible bucker, she had managed to remain in the saddle, putting the cowboys to shame.

Later, in 1904, Bertha became a star performer in Claude William's Show and was a four-time winner in Roman Racing at Pendleton. The spunky Miss Kaelpernick rode under men's rules, was seldom defeated and often beat such cowboys as Ben Corbett and Hoot Gibson.

Four years later Prairie Rose Henderson, an exuberant and talented daughter of a Wyoming rancher, rode to Cheyenne to enter a bronc busting contest. When the lady arrived, she was told, much to her chagrin, that women were not permitted to ride. When Rose demanded to see the rules, she found there was no clause forbidding women to compete, and the officials were forced to let her participate. Her entrance into the arena created a sensation. Women had always been spectators, not competitors, and Miss Henderson was a colorful person. She came dashing out of the chute hanging on with all her strength, and promptly lost the contest. Prairie Rose, however, was really a winner, for she had opened the door to rodeo for other women to follow.

Later, Rose went on to victory in other rodeos and became one of the most flamboyant cowgirls of her era. In 1918, she entered the Gordon, Nebraska, rodeo wearing ostrich plumes over bloomers and a blouse covered with bright sequins she had carefully sewn herself.

Dressing in that manner was unacceptable, but it didn't seem to bother Prairie Rose. She had a large smile and was a popular cowgirl. Her sense of humor was infectious and brought cheer to the other performers.

Rose eventually married a rancher and one cloudy day in 1932, Rose rode off to her last competition. This time, she faced her greatest fear, a storm, and lost her life during a blizzard. Prairie Rose's body was discovered nine years later and identified only by her champion belt buckle. Life for the lady called Rose, was not all roses.

Rodeo was the first sport where women were permitted to compete with males, and those fabulous cowgirls gave it all they had. They rode their hearts out, often dressed in outrageous costumes, and won the applause of the cheering, foot-stomping audience. The sight of a small woman, standing beside a huge animal, never failed to bring a tear to the eye and a roar of admiration from the crowd.

On July 7, 1900, the *New York World* wrote this article describing a beautiful, blonde cowgirl named Lucille Mulhall, "Little Miss Mulhall, who weighs only ninety pounds, can break a bronc, lasso and brand a steer and shoot a coyote at 500 yards. She can also play Chopin, quote Browning, and make mayonnaise."

When that article was written, Lucille was performing with her father, Colonel Zack Mulhall in his famous Wild West Show. They had just completed a mock Indian massacre for the Rough Rider's reunion in Oklahoma City during the time Theodore Roosevelt was a candidate for Vice President of the United States.

"Teddy" Roosevelt was quite impressed with the petite girl. A few days later while visiting the Mulhall ranch, he asked Lucille to put on a roping exhibition for him. When she did as he requested, Roosevelt jokingly said if she could rope a wolf as she had the steer, she could attend the inaugural parade if he was elected. Three hours later Lucille appeared dragging a dead wolf on the end of her lasso, and held the future president to his promise. When President McKinley was assassinated in 1901, Roosevelt became President and Lucille was again invited to the inauguration. This time she had the honor of leading the cowboy band down Pennsylvania Avenue in Washington, D.C.

Lucille was one of the Mulhall's nine children, and at the age of two she was already riding her first horse. It was said she cried to get up on the horse and fussed when she was removed. By her 10th birthday, Lucille could lasso a running jackrabbit and rope a full-grown steer.[1] When her father said she could keep all the calves she roped and branded, the ambitious girl soon had a small herd which she had marked with her own belt buckle.

Mrs. Mulhall did not share her husband's pride in Lucille's skill with the horses. She insisted upon sending her daughter off to a finishing school in St. Louis, but the girl returned within a year. Lucille appeared almost ashamed of the accomplishments she had learned at the school because they were a concession to a world she did not belong in. Lucille was born a cowgirl and determined to reach the top of her profession; anything else merely got in her way.

She became known as "The Darling of the Southwest" and Zack Mulhall built his show around his talented daughter who continued to earn the applause of the spectators. Although Lucille had been taught showmanship by her experienced brothers and sisters, she developed her own unique style and was a real attraction. By the age of 16, Lucille could rope as many as five horses simultaneously. She was one of the few women to wear a divided skirt and refused to ride sidesaddle. The audience loved her anyway, and year after year Miss Mulhall continued to win championship awards. She became the most popular girl in the circuit and was called "The Girl of the Golden West."

In 1902, Lucille broke her leg while appearing at San Antonio. Her adoring fans built a special stand to accommodate her wheelchair and Lucille watched the rodeo in style. Later that evening, her box at the opera house was filled with roses.[2]

Before entering moving pictures, Will Rogers was a trick roper in Zack Mulhall's Show. Lucille often worked with him and they became close friends. He was a shy man and Lucille a quiet girl, they complemented each other in their act, which some said was awesome. The tiny girl, dressed in a long skirt and wearing a feminine hat, let Rogers swing his rope around her. Then she would stand within the loop, a charming captive, creating an appealing picture. Both Will Rogers and Teddy Roosevelt have been credited with giving Lucille the title of "Cowgirl," but whoever said it first said it right. The name stuck and was quite appropriate. The Western horsewomen had always considered themselves cowgirls, but at that point it became official.

Lucille Mulhall, like Will Rogers and Tom Mix, who also rode for Colonel Zack, went on to silent films. Lucille, however, never reached their fame. Her true career was in rodeo and Wild West

[1]**Cowgirl Companion,** by Gail Gilchriest, 1993.
[2]**Those Magnificent Cowgirls: A History of the Rodeo Cowgirls**, by Milt Riske, 1983.

shows where she was known as one of the greatest cowgirls of her era.

Lucille was married twice during her lifetime and in 1945, at the age of 55, she died in an automobile accident near Mulhall, Oklahoma. In 1977, Lucille Mulhall became a Cowgirl Honoree in The National Cowgirl Hall of Fame.

Lorena Trickey, who rode to fame as an all-round champion cowgirl, did not have a supportive family like Lucille Mulhall. She was born in 1893, in Palmer, Oregon, and grew up learning to fend for herself. Her mother died on Lorena's fourth birthday, leaving the girl in the care of her father. She was raised by a series of housekeepers and, as a child, ran wild mustangs over the rugged Oregon countryside with her friends, the Indian children.

"Little" Trickey never grew above five feet or weighed over 100 pounds. She was a lonely girl with long blonde hair, large blue eyes and a rather plain, square face. At an early age, Lorena became fascinated with cowboys and often tried to imitate their skill with the horses. She spent every spare minute hanging around the corrals, determined to become a cowgirl. At the age of 14, Lorena began using the skills she had observed, and with a lot of hard work, she became an accomplished rider.

When Lorena began her career with the rodeo, she was a loner, preferring to keep to herself and avoiding the other rodeo people. She had no close friends and spent all of her time perfecting her skill as a rider. Many of her associates considered the girl hostile, and stayed out of her way. Life was a struggle for her, but she kept striving for success, and it finally came.

In 1919, at the age of 26, Lorena soared to fame at Pendleton, Oregon, as the World's Champion Bronc Riding Cowgirl. She went on to Cheyenne, Wyoming, and walked away with the all-round champion title. To further her rodeo skills, Lorena entered the tougher competition in large cities like Chicago and Denver, where she again rode away with trophies. People began to notice the reserved girl from Oregon, but she was still an avowed loner. The only things that mattered to Miss Trickey were competing and winning.

In 1926, at Pendleton, Lorena had an accident that would have embarrassed many of the other cowgirls, but she took it in stride. She overlapped the other horses, caught her pants on the saddle horn and they dropped to her ankles. With her bare bottom exposed (she had not worn underwear that day) and hanging on for dear life, Lorena attempted to remove her pants. A chivalrous cowboy came to her rescue, whipped off his jacket and wrapped it around the semi-nude girl. Lorena, however, rather than thank him, was furious because he didn't let her finish the race. Several years later, when a rodeo fan remembered her as the girl who lost her pants, Trickey, without batting an eye, replied, "I'm glad you remembered my face."[1]

The year 1926, was laced with trouble for Lorena. She met a rodeo stockman known as "Silent Slim" J.P. Harris, and he swept the little recluse off her feet. They traveled the circuit together and were soon sharing the same bedroom at Trickey's small ranch. One evening, following a performance, the couple became involved in an argument in Trickey's car and Lorena stabbed her lover to death with a pocket knife.

When the police arrested Lorena and took her to jail, she claimed another cowboy, Bob Brown, had been with Slim and her on their drive and that he had stabbed her lover. Brown was taken to jail and cleared of the crime. Lorena then changed her plea to self defense. With tears streaming down her face, she said Harris had attacked her with a wrench because she had been driving recklessly. She fought back, stabbing her lover several times.

Reporters went wild with the story of the famous cowgirl who had become a murderer. One newspaper wrote, with great drama, "Jerking the knife from Slim's now still heart, the distracted girl knelt in the dusty road with Slim's head in her lap and arms around his shoulders sobbed." At the trial, however, Lorena was found innocent. Racehorse owners and fans had provided money for her defense and a rodeo stockman came forward to tell the jury of many beatings Lorena had suffered at the hands of her lover.

Following the trial, Lorena attempted to pick up the pieces of her life. She did trick riding and racing in California and the Midwest, and even won a few trophies, but once a rodeo star lost her reputation, it was hard to regain it. Lorena went to Hollywood and began performing dangerous stunts for the movies. She doubled for Mary Pickford and worked with Tom Mix. Trickey even tried vaudeville with her trick horse, Black Baby, but life was never to be the same.

In 1928, at the age of 35, Lorena, met Magnus "Pete" Peterson, and became his business partner in a racing stable. Pete was a former cowboy and together they trained their own horses. With a little work, Lorena became a good jockey and started racing at the smaller

[1]**Rodeo World & Western Heritage**, 1979.

tracks and in local rodeos. She married Pete a few months later, but bad luck still plagued the former champion. Disaster struck again when a train carrying their fine racehorses was derailed, killing or crippling most of their stock.

Miss Trickey made her last professional ride at Klamath Falls, and retired with her husband to Tonopah, Nevada, where they became prospectors. Lorena Trickey died in 1961, at the age of 67. The girl who was once the winner of the McAlpin Trophy as the World's Greatest Cowgirl was buried among the old-timers in the small cemetery at Tonopah.

Vera McGinnis, known as "Vera Mac," was considered one of the most daring and talented cowgirls of the early rodeo era. She brought the romance of the Wild West to other countries and, like Annie Oakley, Vera always thrilled her audience.

Vera was born in 1894, on a small ranch in East Lynn, Missouri, the daughter of Dr. and Mrs. R.W. McGinnis. Her early years were spent roaming the range on the bare back of a burro with cropped ears, who became her first baby-sitter. Although money was scarce in the McGinnis family, her parents eventually managed to buy Vera a mustang named "Cricket," and her famous career began.

At the age of 13, the girl entered her first competition on the back of her own mustang wearing a homemade outfit and, to everyone's surprise, won the women's open race. Five years later, Vera was working as a secretary when a traveling rodeo came to town. She entered a relay race and won, and when the rodeo left town, Vera went with it.

The slim, blonde woman soon learned that life in the rodeo was not all glamour, it was hard, dirty work. She weighed only 110 pounds, but had to lift a 20 pound saddle, maintain her own horse and received no guaranteed wage, just a percentage. In order to make travel expenses, Vera quickly established herself as a trick rider so she could enter more than one event. This meant more entry fees and new outfits, and, the competition was fierce in the arena. Vera had entered a new world that reeked of horse sweat, dust, and manure, and she learned to love it. She soon earned the respect of the other riders and acquired the nickname of "Little Mac."

When Vera joined Barney Sherry's troupe and headed for the stampede at Winnipeg, Canada, she was a hard, tough cowgirl who knew her way around the world of rodeo. One of her best-known stunts was acting like a drunken cowboy, whooping and hollering, while standing up in the saddle with a bottle in her hand.[1] Her most thrilling act was when she crawled beneath the horse's stomach while traveling at a fast gallop.

The shows came quickly for Little Mac, she performed in Cheyenne, Calgary, Pendleton and the biggest of them all, Madison Square Garden in New York. Vera had become an expert at relay, trick riding, bucking bulls and Roman racing — and she was winning. Mac wore leather skirts with velvet bloomers, then branched out to divided skirts, tied below her knees. She was always careful not to expose any part of her leg which, no matter how comfortable, would have been unacceptable. It all paid off, for Vera Mac was awarded the title of Best Dressed Cowgirl.

Eventually, Little Mac lost her heart to a jaunty cowboy from Nevada, Earl Simpson, and as they traveled together, love bloomed and wedding bells rang. Following their marriage, the couple briefly settled on a ranch in Montana, using the money from occasional rodeo appearances to supplement their meager income. Vera loved the ranch, but Earl preferred rodeo, so she left Montana behind and returned to the circuit. By that time the other cowgirls had become adventurous and were wearing boots or rubber soled tennis shoes, but none were brave enough to wear pants.

When Vera returned to the rodeo, her attitude was different. She said, "I don't care what I do as long as I can do it on horseback."[2] This was a hard period in Vera's life; she had to get established again and there was very little money to do it with. Once Mac hid in a railroad car with the horses to save money. Another time a strained ligament temporarily slowed her down, but she bounced back and did trick riding for the Ringling Brothers and Barnum and Bailey Circus for a season.

Earl and Vera began moving in different directions and soon drifted from their marriage. Little Mac began working alone. She followed the round-ups and frontier celebrations and, at a Fort Worth Show, became the first cowgirl to appear in public wearing men's trousers. She had removed the fly and fastened them on the right side. Other cowgirls soon adapted trousers, but they had to sew their own or hire a seamstress, as no one manufactured them.

In 1924, at the age of 30, Vera joined Tex Austin's troupe and went to Europe. Austin paid only the fare over. It was understood the entertainers were on their own and kept what they won; and they did well. At the British Empire Exhibition, the cowgirls were magnifi-

[1]The Saga of Vera Mac, The Western Horseman, January 1969.
[2]ibid

cent in their bright Western outfits. The people were so excited they greeted the performers with wild applause and the horsewomen were written about in every newspaper. They wined and dined with the royal family and went on to play the London Coliseum, which had the largest stage in the world at the time. Vera traveled to Dublin, Ireland, where she received a Loving Cup, and in France the troupe played to a packed arena. When the cowgirls arrived in the Orient, cheering crowds filled every seat.

Vera made two tours to Europe and the Orient. On her second tour, she caught the eye of a sultan who was captivated when she appeared in a white satin suit with pants laced up the side with a silver cord, a sleeveless bolero trimmed in gold and silver braid, bright red blouse and sash, and, a white Stetson hat.[1] When he invited her to visit his home, Little Mac almost didn't go as she was afraid he would put her in his harem. The sultan, however, was a perfect gentleman and Vera left with a beautiful bracelet he had created for her from a boar's tusk.

When she returned to America, Vera had a fling in Hollywood where she doubled for Mary Pickford and Norma Talmadge. She also starred in a series of two-reelers that were full of horses and action. In 1931, Vera met and married her second husband, Homer Ferra, a horse trainer. She continued on with her life in rodeo and he traveled with the troupe, taking care of Vera's horses.

Unfortunately, Mac's career ended in 1934 during an exhibition at Livermore, California, when her horse fell and rolled in front of 20,000 spectators. Vera was thrown into a broken heap and suffered from a collapsed lung, broken hip, back and ribs. She was not expected to live, but being a tough little fighter, Vera fought to regain her health and managed to ride again for a brief time.

She eventually had to give up the rodeo and settled down with her husband raising and training horses. When Vera McGinnis died in 1991, she was one month short of her 97th birthday.

Vera Mac wasn't the only cowgirl to be thrown to the ground in a broken heap. Accidents were part of the rodeo and the women lived with constant danger. They suffered bruises, sprains, broken bones and often death rode as their companion.

In 1929, Bonnie McCarrol received fatal injuries at Pendleton because she could not free herself from the hobbled stirrups. During her violent ride, she lost her hold on the reins and was whipped over and over again. When Bonnie's feet finally broke lose, she was

[1]**Rodeo Road: My Life as a Pioneer Cowgirl**, by Vera McGinnis, 1974.

slammed to the ground and died eight days later. Most women bronc riders rode with a hobble, which meant a piece of leather was tied under the horse from one stirrup to the other. This made it easier for the girl to remain in the saddle. However, many times the hobble was dangerous; the rider could not get her feet loose as illustrated in the unfortunate death of Bonnie McCarrol.

These women were so intoxicated by their profession, they seldom gave in to injuries. Tad Lucas was going under her horse's belly in a trick riding contest at the Chicago World's Fair when she slipped and was caught up in the galloping hooves for several minutes. She finally broke free only to find her arm was severely broken. The doctor wanted to remove the arm, but Tad wouldn't hear of it. A few months later, she was trick riding with the arm in a cast and within three years she was back on a bronc.

When Fox Hastings's horse fell on her during a Kansas City Roundup, everyone thought her neck was broken. She was carried from the arena on a stretcher, only to return a few minutes later riding in an open car, waving and smiling at the spectators. A roar could be heard from the crowd as the gallant lady mounted her horse to complete the ride and gave a perfect performance. No one in the audience knew she collapsed a few minutes later in agony and was unable to perform for several days. A cowgirl always felt she had to finish her ride — unless she was dead!

Fox Hastings went on to become one of the few women bulldoggers of her day. Needless to say, she also endured many more bone-jarring injuries before ending her career. Fox took her own life one lonely night in a barren hotel room in Phoenix, Arizona. Her luck had run out.

Few cowgirls could compete with men when it came to bulldogging and steer wrestling. They were too slight to go hand to horn with a 750-pound steer.[1] Although many attempted the feat, few were successful. The girl who brought the steer down, however, always won a standing ovation from the audience in appreciation of her showmanship and bravery.

Women excelled at horse racing, trick riding and relay. Their weight was an advantage and, due to their gentler nature, the females seemed to have a closer kinship with the horses. It was not uncommon to see a large animal respond to a diminutive cowgirl's whispered command or her soft touch.

The appropriate attire society expected the early cowgirls to wear

[1]**Cowgirl Companion**, by Gail Gilchriest, 1993.

often hampered their riding skills and caused accidents. While men dressed in protective pants and wore high-heeled boots that helped keep their feet in the stirrups, the women wore long skirts which were constantly in the way. What the women lacked in comfort, though, they made up for in color. Cowgirls livened their attire with bright bandannas, silk scarves around their waists and the more daring put a fancy feather in their hats.

As the full skirt became divided and reached the boots, the girls began adding sequins or beads to their vests. Some wore their skirts over outrageous bloomers made of satin and silks. Others threw caution to the wind and appeared in everything flamboyant, from ostrich feathers to rhinestones. In 1927, Vera Mac shocked the public when she wore pants, and Ruth Roach added hearts to her boots, which was considered scandalous. But, Kitty Canutt took it one step further when she had a diamond set into a front tooth. The tooth served many purposes. It attracted attention and, when she was down on her luck, Kitty could always pawn it for an entry fee.

With all their color and talent, these marvelous ladies added a special touch to the Grand Entry. A beautiful cowgirl would lead the procession carrying "Old Glory," with her high-stepping horse prancing to the rhythm of the National Anthem. As the spectators rose to their feet, magnificently attired cowboys and cowgirls came riding in greeted by thunderous applause — it was always a stirring moment and set the pace for the excitement that lay ahead.

While the thrill and pageantry of the rodeos and Wild West Shows caught the attention of America, pulp magazines, radio programs and silent movies were not far behind. Many of the handsome cowboys began making Westerns, trading the range for a ride across the silent screen. Although the cowboy always won the heart of his fair lady, the cowgirl rarely won anything, especially her man. It was still a man's world and, unless they were already stars, women were expected to be stunt riders and stand-ins or simply disappear into the sunset, alone. Very few cowgirls became famous.

Despite their lack of fame in Hollywood, the American cowgirls rode on to victory, carrying the banner of freedom into the future. They were the spirit of the early frontier, bigger than life, and a legend of the West.

Courtesy of the Buffalo Bill Cody Historical Center

Miss Annie Oakley

Sketches of the Wild West Show

Buffalo Bill returned to Earl's court, the scene of his former triumphs in London, after a long European tour . . . An added interest to the present Wild West show lies in the fact that Colonel Cody is accompanied by twenty military hostages, Indians engaged in the late rising (by permission of his Government). There are between sixty and seventy Indians altogether, . . . who take part in the present exhibition.

The merits of the show rest solely upon its natural features, and not upon any artificial aids. The Indians are Indians in their warpaint and feathers, and the horses are the Mexican mustangs and "broncos" of the plains, while the horsemanship is so undeniable good that a succession of visits does not pall upon the spectator.

Our sketches severally illustrate some of the more remarkable incidents; for example, the mounting in hot haste of the Pony Express, showing the method by which letters and dispatches of the republic were formerly carried across the vast American continent previous to the introduction of railways and telegraphs. Hunting the buffalo in the Far West, a scene of sufficient realism, considering these same buffaloes are hunted twice a day; it is even possible they may enjoy it as a rough and tumble game, seeing that they do not get killed. Lassoing horses is another interesting feature.

In addition to these, there is the remarkable shooting of Miss Annie Oakley, whose expertness with the rifle is phenomenal; an attack on a emigrant train by Indians, which is decidedly picturesque; the capture of the Deadwood mail coach and subsequent rescue by Buffalo Bill and his Cowboys, and some clever sharp-shooting by the redoubtable Colonel himself. It is a exciting program, admirably carried out, and well managed by all concerned. The whole party are encamped in the grounds adjoining the arena, and the Indians and their painted tents provide a never failing source of interest to the visitors, who crowd the sidewalks of an afternoon after the exhibition is over.

— The Queen, The Lady's Newspaper, May 28, 1892

Courtesy of Buffalo Bill Cody Historical Center, Cody, WY

Lucille Mulhall

America's first lady steer roper.

Lucille performed and competed in Wild West shows beginning in the early 1900s.

Bertha Kaelpernick

Bertha was one of the first women to ride in a rodeo and often rode under men's rules.

Courtesy of the Wyoming State Museum

Mabel Strickland

She was Queen of the 1927 Pendleton Round-Up and rode to fame as an All-Round Cowgirl.

Courtesy of the Wyoming State Museum

Lorena Trickey

Winner of the McAlpin Trophy

Prairie Rose Henderson
She was one of the most flamboyant cowgirls of her era.

"Here we come!"

Vera McGinnis and Bonnie McCarroll

Bonnie McCarroll

Thrown from her horse "Silver" at Pendelton in 1929.
She died from the fall eight days later.

Margie Wright

*Margie lost her life in the arena when her horse fell over backward
and she fractured her head on a fence.*

Lotta Crabtree

*Little Lotta danced her way through the mining camps
and towns of the West into the heart of America.*

Chapter 3

A LITTLE DIVERSION

I n 1864, the Gold Hill News, in Nevada, wrote with enthusiasm: *"She has Come!—The Menken was aboard one of the pioneer coaches which reached Gold Hill this morning at half-past eleven o'clock. She is decidedly a pretty little woman, and judging by her style, we suppose she does not care how she rides—as she was on the front seat with her back turned to the horses. She will doubtless draw large houses in Virginia City . . ."* And indeed, the entire town turned out to see the famous Adah Isaacs Menken, a woman who was recognized as America's first pin-up girl and whose toast to the Victorian public was "Marry young and often."

Adah Menken, at the age of 26, was considered incomparable in the role of "Mezeppa." Her almost nude femininity shocked the audiences as she allowed herself to be lashed to the back of a stallion, wearing only flesh-colored tights and a wisp of loincloth. It was thought to be the most daring act ever performed by a woman, as both horse and rider had to play their part to perfection; Adah was often injured during her performances.

"The Menken" was on her way to appear at Maguire's Opera house in Virginia City, Nevada, the Queen of the Comstock. Virginia City was a place where ordinary men became overnight millionaires, while others died with their faces in the mud, clutching a piece of worthless rock. Those who were successful clamored for amusement, so in 1863, Tom Maguire, a San Francisco impresario, opened Virginia City's first opera house. "Maguire's" was as garish and gaudy as its performers, which ranged from Adah Menken to minstrels and dog fights. John Piper acquired the theater in 1868 and changed the name to Piper's. He brought in fresh new talent and top entertainers and, under his ownership, it became one of the most impressive theaters in the West.

Many exciting women appeared at Piper's Opera House. The deliciously naughty Lola Montez performed her wicked Spider Dance upon the ornate stage and drove the audience wild. Glamorous Lillie Langtry graced Piper's with her wit and beauty. Lillie, always a lady, initiated the Red Carpet treatment when she refused to dirty her dainty slippers on Virginia City's muddy streets. And, lovely Caroline Chapman, the "Sweetheart of the West," brought her own special warmth to both the opera house and the local population.

Although these talented ladies of the theater were all great entertainers who earned a fortune off the larger cities of America, they never failed to reach out to the smaller towns of the West. It was there, in those out of the way places, they brought a bit of relaxation and joy—and it was there they were loved and needed, for life on the frontier was never easy.

The western experience of the 1850s may have been exciting to a few woman, but for the majority, it was a back-breaking attempt for survival, with little reward. They worked from sunrise to late in the night, struggling to scratch a meager living from the land. The western woman suffered from overwork, childbirth and a terrible loneliness that was part of the vast new country that surrounded her. The sight of a visitor, who for a few brief minutes would provide companionship, was always a welcome one. Both the men and women needed a bit of diversion, and fortunately it arrived many years before Buffalo Bill Cody and his Wild West Show.

The first to liven the dreary frontier were the traveling minstrels. These hardy men braved dangerous mountains and arid plains to spread cheer and earn a few dollars. They performed on the floor of a blacksmith's shop, schoolroom, tent or saloon. The "band" usually consisted of a flute, violin and guitar, played by musicians who never learned to read a note.

Their lack of professionalism, however, did not deter the enthusiastic settlers and miners. They welcomed any form of amusement and would travel for hours, in all kinds of weather, to listen and dance to the wild, carefree beat of the music. Care-worn housewives shed their weariness, put on a fancy gown and a ribbon in their hair to whirl the night away. It was a time to see and be seen, and, for the single person, it was an opportunity to meet a future mate.

The minstrels were soon followed by more professional troupes, offering everything from medicine shows to drama and variety. The famous Lotta Crabtree was one of the earliest comediennes to become part of a traveling company. In the 1850s, at the age of seven, she began touring the Sierra Nevada Mountains of California and Nevada, bringing cheer to the lonely miners. Her bright red curls, deep infectious laughter and nimble feet never failed to delight the audience. At the end of her act, she was always rewarded with gold nuggets and valuable trinkets, which the child quickly scooped into her shoe.

Lotta laughed and danced her way through the mining camps and towns, then went on to San Francisco, where she performed at the leading theaters. Her chaperone was her mother, Mary Ann Crabtree, a severe woman who carefully watched over both the girl and her money.

Lotta never enjoyed a happy childhood. She was not allowed to have friends and grew up with a rigorous work routine that few adults could endure. Even in her late teens, Lotta's mother refused to let her attend the offstage parties or participate in anything frivolous.

At the age of 17, Miss Lotta wore hoop-skirts which showed her knees, and when she smoked cigarettes on stage, she was comical. She could roll off a sofa, expose more than a slim ankle, and be hilarious. In the fight for top billing, she fought with all the vitality her small body could gather. The audiences loved her as though she were their own creation.

As Lotta's success continued to grow, Mary Ann decided they should move to New York so the girl could go on to greater fame. Lotta had been singing and dancing for 10 years without a break, and she was financially well off. Her mother had invested Lotta's money carefully, so carefully that her daughter did not own a silk dress until she was 21.

Although Lotta was exhausted and showed signs of depression, she put her own feelings behind and followed her mother's wishes. Soon she was romping her way through difficult parts. She played the biggest houses to delighted audiences and rose to fame and riches, just as Mary Ann had wanted.

Life for Lotta, however, was never to be a happy one. She put her love, or need, for her mother and the theater, before any love she might have felt for a man. There was no romance and marriage was out of the question. Lotta was adored by her fans, but lacked personal relationships. When she died in 1924, at the age of 77, Lotta left an estate valued at $4 million to strangers. The little girl, with the bright red curls, who had brought so much cheer to the West, died a sad and lonely death.[1]

Few cities in the west were able to afford the opulence of Piper's Opera House. In the sparsely settled Plains and Rockies, crude buildings were the primary places of entertainment. The communities were simply too small to support a theater. It was not uncommon to see an enthusiastic group of thespians helping the local citizens erect a temporary playhouse. Although the actresses in these areas were generally less sophisticated than those in the larger cities, what they lacked in sophistication, they more than made up for in talent and exuberance.

Della Pringle, a beautiful, blue-eyed blonde with shapely legs, was one of the many actresses to travel the kerosene footlight circuit during the late 1800s. She was known both as "Jolly" Della and the owner of The Pringle Company, a small troupe of talented actors who played the rural communities and army posts of the West.

Miss Pringle was born in 1870 in Iowa. By the time she was eight years old, she had already made her first appearance as "Little Eva" in a hometown production of "Uncle Tom's Cabin." This was the beginning of a love affair with the theater that lasted 35 years and became the most important part of Della's life. She spent her childhood playing in a series of short-run engagements and left home at the age of 19, with high-hopes of conquering the entertainment world.

Della worked hard and saved her money. After a 40-week straight run, she started her own small company with a few entertainers who were popular for their clean, lively comedy. They traveled the cowtowns of the frontier by stagecoach and performed wherever there was a group of interested people and an empty building. Once, in Wyoming, the troupe put on a play in a hotel dining room, using the pantry for their many quick changes. Della created all the costumes. She was handy with a needle and could whip out fashionable gowns from silks and satins that were bought at bargain prices.

As the company traveled from town to camp, Della Pringle became one of the brightest stars on the circuit. Her songs were delightful, and when she appeared in her short skirt, Della livened every performance. Although Della and her company were popular, they had to learn to deal with adversities as well as successes. There were rough towns with tough characters, and, unfortunately, more lean days than fat ones. But no one considered leaving the theater, it

[1]**Women of the Sierra,** by Anne Seagraves, 1990.

would be like committing suicide, for acting was in their blood.

The company made their first appearance in Boise, Idaho, in 1900, in the old Pinney Theater. Della never forgot the friendly town and returned there many times during her career; she was always sure of a warm welcome and good press releases.

In 1905, Della received a real break when her company played the ornate Tabor Opera House in Leadville, Colorado. Their reception was outstanding and the audience enthusiastic — Della in the role of the tragic "Camille," was so believable there wasn't a dry eye in the theater, especially among the prostitutes, who wept openly. She was invited to appear on Broadway, and temporarily left her troupe. Broadway, however, was not one of Della's successes, and she soon rejoined her company, leaving the bustle and bright lights behind. She was happy to be back with people who appreciated her, singing and dancing in the frontier towns she loved so much.

For the next 15 years, the Pringle Company was successful in the Black Hills of the Dakotas and the smaller towns further west. But Della was growing older, and the hard schedule and constant travel soon became too strenuous for her to handle. The era of the silent screen had arrived, so she struck out alone to make a brief appearance in the movies. Unfortunately, Della, like most other actresses, did not make the grade.

With very little money in her purse, she went to work for the Mack Sennett Company Players and tried her hand at slapstick. Although her pride was often wounded when a pie hit her in the face, she preferred the pie to unemployment. When the Sennett Players folded, Della made a last desperate try in the tent shows, but her days of glory were over—Miss Pringle was broke.

She borrowed money from a friend and returned to Boise, the town that had always been so friendly. With her last few dollars, Della managed to lease an old run-down boarding house, rolled up her sleeves and made the place livable. She soon filled the rooms with old actors and began renting her beautiful costumes for amateur plays and masquerade parties. Della even managed to perform in a few local productions.

When her health began to fail, Della was forced to close her boarding house and sell her vast wardrobe. Ill, and without a family, her last years were spent living on state old age benefits in a small apartment at the County Hospital in Boise, with cherished photos and scrapbooks of her memorable past. When Della Pringle died in

1952 at the age of 82, there was no one left to mourn her passing.

"Jolly" Della, however, has not been forgotten. Old playbills and programs of her happier days in the theater can still be found in the smaller towns of the early frontier. At Tabor's Opera House in Leadville, the Pringle Company's name is listed among the many famous personalities to grace its stage. The old Opera House, like Della Pringle, was part of the history of the west, and it too has its own fascinating story.

The Tabor Opera House was built by early-day mining czar Horace Tabor, who climbed from obscurity to riches beyond his wildest dreams. The magnificent structure, constructed in 1879, was Tabor's first valuable possession and, at that time, the finest theater in Colorado. Its furnishings were the most expensive money could buy and although the seating capacity was 880, it was said there wasn't a bad seat in the house. The color scheme of red, gold, white and sky-blue, accentuated by 72 jet gas lights, further enhanced the splendor of the establishment. It was a first-class entertainment center, dedicated to the legitimate theater and the pride of Leadville. The Opera House, however, was more than a place of entertainment, it was part of the intriguing "Tabor Triangle," a story of wealth, love and sadness.

Horace Tabor was originally a stonecutter from Vermont. In 1857, at the age of 27, he married Augusta Pierce and, like many others, they traveled West to seek their fortune. Their first home was a dilapidated farm in Kansas, where Augusta gave birth to a son. When news of the fabulous gold strikes reached them, Tabor realized they would never get rich in Kansas and took his wife and son further west.

Tabor followed the drifting population and eventually ended up prospecting in Colorado. He was not successful, but Augusta managed to keep the family going by baking fresh bread and pies for the miners. Tabor finally gave up prospecting and opened a store and Augusta began a small bank. The miners needed someone to watch over their valuables and they knew she was an honest woman.

The Tabors moved their business wherever there was a boomtown, and in 1879, they were in Leadville, Colorado. People traveled for miles to shop at their store. Augusta was known for her kindness, she never turned a hungry person away, and Tabor was a generous man who grubstaked many miners down on their luck. One day, when two poor prospectors walked in and asked for a loan, it was only natural that they would receive it. Tabor gave them $17 in return for a third of their earnings, and a week later, they struck a vein called the Little Pittsburgh—a year later, Tabor cleared over a million dollars and the triangle began.

With the money from the Little Pittsburgh, Tabor began investing in other mines, including the Matchless, which cost $170,000 and netted him $1,000 a day. It would seem Horace Tabor had acquired the "Midas Touch," for everything he bought made him wealthier. Augusta, however, was not happy. She was a simple, hard-working woman and not used to riches. When Tabor built her a mansion, she was reluctant to enter, and when she did, Augusta preferred the servants quarters to her luxurious suite. Perhaps Augusta had a premonition of disaster, she knew that easy money could be lost just as easily as it came, and she began to drift apart from her husband.

Meanwhile, Tabor kept spending, and then he met Elizabeth "Baby" Doe, a beautiful young divorcee who left Oshkosh, Wisconsin, for the boomtown of Leadville. Baby Doe had heard of Tabor and his new found wealth, and set out to catch him. What she didn't expect, however, was such a charming man. Although Tabor was middle-aged, he was quite distinguished looking in his carefully tailored suit with diamond cuff links and ring. Baby Doe felt his power and kindness, and, to her surprise, she found the man attractive and irresistible.

Baby Doe swept Tabor off his feet and without batting an eye, he divorced Augusta, the woman who had stood by his side during the many hard years. There was no way the older woman could compete with the stately, young charmer who many claimed was the handsomest woman in Colorado. When Augusta accepted Tabor's settlement of $30,000, she turned to the judge and asked if she could keep the Tabor name. Upon hearing she could, the unhappy woman said, "I will, it is mine until I die," and left in tears.[1]

Baby Doe and Horace Tabor were married in an elaborate ceremony in Washington, D.C., her gown cost $7,000. Many politicians attended the wedding, but their wives refused the invitations. Tabor bought his bride magnificent mansions and covered her with expensive jewelry, but no woman ever came to visit, for the new Mrs. Tabor was not accepted by society. Mrs. Augusta Tabor was still considered to be "Leadville's First Lady."

During the next few years, Baby Doe bore two daughters and in

[1]**The Miners**, Time Life Books, 1976.

their own way the Tabors were happy. However, their prosperity was not to last as, unfortunately, Augusta was right in her skepticism. Ten years after their marriage, Tabor lost his wealth during the panic of 1893, when the price of silver dropped to less than the cost of mining it. Tabor had spent, or given away, most of his money and he was broke at 63 years old. All of his friends waited for his lovely young wife to leave, but she didn't. Baby Doe had developed a special love for her husband and she remained by his side. The family moved to cheap lodgings in one of the hotels Tabor had once owned. From their windows they could look out at the grandeur that once was theirs.

When Augusta heard about Tabor's lost fortune, she offered to help, but neither her ex-husband nor his wife would accept her generosity. Augusta had always lived modestly and invested her money wisely, she had accumulated a small fortune of her own. Ever since the divorce she had waited and hoped that someday her husband would return, now she knew he never would.

Tabor went back to work and attempted to make a comeback, but he had lost the "Midas" touch. In 1898, he was appointed Postmaster of Denver, and died the following year leaving Baby Doe alone and penniless with two daughters to care for. The only thing Tabor left was the Matchless Mine in Leadville. His last words to her were to hang on to the mine for there was a fortune in silver to be found there, and she believed him.

Baby Doe sold what was left of her belongings and jewelry. She moved with her daughters into a one-room shack near the mine and set up housekeeping. When her daughters grew up and left, she remained behind guarding the mine with a rifle. Baby Doe refused to let anyone, other than herself, touch the mine and spent the rest of her life waiting for the silver to flow as it had before. She was desperately poor and wore old, ragged clothing with gunny sacks around her feet, but would not accept charity. Her brother arranged with the grocer to let her have what she needed. Baby Doe, however, never knew about it. When she went to the store for her meager supply of food, she would always tell the grocer she would pay when the Matchless came in.

Baby Doe never gave up hope. Old friends of her husband kept her supplied with firewood, but the proud woman used only a few sticks. She died quietly one day in 1935; her body was discovered several days later frozen in the lonely shack. Baby Doe, one of the most sought-after women in Colorado, had remained true to her husband and his Matchless Mine.

The Opera House was the last of Horace Tabor's possessions to be sold. Although there were many changes in management, the doors always remained open. The years of its heyday were filled with numerous variety acts, popular plays and the finest entertainers of the day. Famous stars like Lillian Russell, Maude Adams and Anna Held, a Ziegfeld beauty, played the Tabor Opera House during their Western tours.

One can only imagine the excitement of seeing Lillian Russell appear upon that large stage singing and dancing in musicals such as "Whirl-i-gig" and "Fiddle-dee-dee." Lillian, a corn-fed American girl from Iowa, became the ideal of her generation. Her peaches-and-cream complexion, hourglass figure and startling blue eyes radiated an earthy magnetism that kept the audience in the palm of her hand. When she walked on stage wearing a pair of purple tights that displayed more than a little of her shapely legs, the theatergoers went wild.

Miss Russell represented all that was glamorous. She was known for her enormous plumed hats, voluptuous figure and exquisitely jeweled gowns. Wealthy men like Diamond Jim Brady showered her path with diamonds and her lovely voice and natural charm carried Lillian to the top of her profession. She became the highest paid actress of the era, yet managed to remain unspoiled and generous.

With all her success, though, Lillian had one big flaw, her taste in men was extremely poor. Her first husband was a worthless unemployed musician, the second a bigamist, and her third a small, well-known matinee idol who humiliated Miss Russell before the world. When the press ruthlessly tore Lillian apart, she fled to her friend Jim Brady for comfort. Brady was the one man she could rely upon; their companionship was never one of a physical nature, it was always platonic. To her, he was living proof that all men were not scoundrels, and their friendship lasted a lifetime.

Although Miss Russell enjoyed many honors during her career, one of the most exciting happened in 1890, when her voice was the first to be heard over the new long-distance telephone. On a special line from her dressing room in New York City to Washington D.C., she sang a song from the "Grand Dutchess." What a thrill Lillian's clear soprano voice must have been to President Harrison, who was listening on the other end.

Miss Russell was admired for her talent as well as her love of America. In an era when French clothing was considered to be the most stylish, she insisted all of her costumes be made by her own country's designers. When the curtain rose on Lillian Russell's San Francisco performance of "La Cigale," it was said that France could not claim a share in the lovely creations that adorned the famous star. For the first time, a French opera was interpreted by an American woman wearing American gowns. It is easy to understand why the lady was adored by her many fans.

Lillian Russell remained America's sweetheart for 43 years and at the age of 57, she gracefully retired from the stage. When Miss Russell made her final farewell, she appeared before a packed house wearing a magnificently plumed hat and an elaborately jeweled gown. The audience solemnly rose to their feet to pay tribute to the golden lady of the American theater who had brightened the lives of thousands of ordinary people.

Maude Adams, a delightful western actress, visited Tabor's Opera House many times during her illustrious career. The Discovery of Programs lists a few of the plays Miss Adams made popular; "The Midnight Bell;" "The Little Minister;" "The Old Curiosity Shop" and a little sketch, "Hop'O Me Thumb," which she did as a curtain-opener. Unfortunately, the dates of her appearances are missing.

Maude was the daughter of Annie Adams, a noted leading lady of the stage, and she followed in her mother's footsteps. At the age of six, she was already a professional actress who had no trouble learning her lines and was called a "Little Artist." The precocious child found the theater to be an exciting game of make-believe and was used to being treated as an adult. Because Maude had nothing in common with other children, she preferred the company of older people and found the classroom a bother. It wasn't until she was too old to be considered a child actress that life became a serious affair.

Maude was a slight young woman with huge blue eyes, an elfish, bewitching face and pleasing personality. At the age of 15, her mother arranged for her to become an apprentice in a traveling stock company and the next few years were spent touring the smaller communities of the West. During this time, Maude began to realize the importance of comedy, and she accepted the lighter side of drama for her career.

Her mischievous charm and talent carried Maude to the bright lights of New York, and in 1905, she became the first American actress to play the leading role in "Peter Pan." During the play's three straight years on Broadway, Miss Adams became the idol of thousands; it was the successful role of Peter Pan that made her famous. Several years after the show closed, Maude took it on the Silver Circuit and played her celebrated role throughout the West.

When Maude Adams retired at the age of 51, "Peter Pan" continued to entertain audiences around the world. It has been made into movies and plays, and, in 1953, Walt Disney produced the original show in a full-length animated cartoon. "Peter Pan" is considered one of the most loved plays of the 20th century, and the legacy of the talented actress who started it on the road to fame.

Anna Held, one of the loveliest entertainers to visit the West, brought the glamour of the Follies to the stage at the old Opera House. Miss Held was discovered by Florenz Ziegfeld in 1897 when she was singing in a French music hall. Ziegfeld was immediately attracted to the talented young woman and brought her to America. With the great Ziegfeld behind her, Anna became an overnight star. He was an expert at creating beautiful women and Miss Held was a natural. She had an 18-inch waist, light brown hair and enough spice to be considered naughty.

Ziegfeld dressed her in dainty lace undergarments, exquisite gowns that billowed out around her tiny waist, and covered her with expensive jewels. She wore shoes with silver heels studded in diamonds and rubies and always managed to let a bit of lace peak out from under her fancy gown. Anna became a petite bundle of delight who could hold her own among the most beautiful Ziegfeld girls. When she sang "Won't You Come Play Wiz Me," Anna sparkled and the audience cheered—they couldn't get enough!

When Ziegfeld informed the press that Anna took daily milk baths to keep her body creamy and white, thousands of women ran to the store to buy milk. Everything Miss Held did, they copied. Lacy undergarments became the rage and whenever she changed the style of her clothing, dressmakers struggled to imitate the Anna Held look. Ziegfeld cleverly added novel touches to Anna's wardrobe and dreamed up new escapades for his little creation, then shared them with the public.

Anna and Ziegfeld were married a few months after she arrived in America, and for the next few years, they were very much in love. Anna traveled with the follies and in 1904, she starred in Ziegfeld's "Mamselle Napoleon" at Tabor's Opera House. It was the most dazzling spectacular Leadville had ever seen, and little Anna became the toast of the West.

Ziegfeld lavished his wealth and time on Anna and led her on to become one of the most celebrated women of the day. Then he lost interest in his wife and began paying more attention to his shows. Their marriage came to an end in 1912, when Anna filed for divorce. She left New York and began touring the West while her husband surrounded himself with glamorous girls and the glitter of his Follies.[1]

Following the divorce, Anna returned many times to Leadville. During her last appearance in 1918, she was in poor health and had to be carried from her hotel to the theater, then rested on a couch between acts. The audience never knew the little actress wasn't well as she managed to put on an exceptional performance.[2]

Shortly after leaving Leadville, Anna died from what was described as too much dieting and cinching in of her waist. When Miss Held knew the end was near, she called for the only man she had ever loved. Unfortunately Florenz Ziegfeld arrived too late to say goodbye to the woman he had once adored; Anna died alone.

The old-time entertainers brought excitement and fantasy to the stage that enabled the pioneers to forget their hardships and difficult existence. They presented a make-believe world and offered more than a little diversion to the early West. Fortunately, many of the old theaters with colorful memories of yesterday have been preserved through the years. In Leadville, Colorado, the old Tabor Opera House is being restored under the loving care of Mrs. Evelyn Furman, its sixth owner. She has carefully preserved the history of the theater with programs, posters and portraits from her private collection which line the walls of the foyer. The past may be gone—but it has not been forgotten.

[1]**The Ziegfeld Follies,** by Marjorie Farnsworth, 1956.
[2]**The Tabor Opera House:** A Captivating History, by Evelyn F. Livingston Furman, 1984.

The Tabor Opera House
Leadville, Colorado
Opened November 20, 1879

The Tabor Opera House in Leadville, is one of the noted historical attractions of Colorado. It is rich in the culture of a fabulous era and a place where the visitor is transported back to the glamor of a time when life ran the gamut from the raw to the sublime . . . During its heyday many famous stars traveled to Leadville. They were paid handsome salaries and basked in the adulation given them by the entertainment-starved people who had silver to spend lavishly.

On opening night "The Serious Family" was received by thunderous applause. It was followed by popular plays of the day like "The Silver Slipper" and "Bohemian Girl." But, Florenz Ziegfeld's "Mamselle Napoleon," starring Anna Held, was hailed as one of the greatest productions. The dazzling performance was unsurpassed in beauty of setting, glittering splendor and exquisite wardrobe.

The stage of the famous Opera House was graced by actors and actresses who had attained distinction. It was on the "Silver Circuit" out of New York, which employed only the very best entertainment. Leading roles were played by those of the legitimate theater. A few of the celebrated artists were Otis Skinner, Laurence Barrett and Helena Modjeska . . .Other acclaimed attractions were Sousa's Marine Band, The Royal Canadians and Al Field's Minstrels. Even the Great Houdini once thrilled the audience with his magic.

Although the era of the once famous Opera House is over, guests visiting today do not merely stand at a barred doorway. Literally speaking, they are invited to see the "last show" in a beautiful building. Large framed photographs, autographed by renowned entertainers, hang on the high walls in the foyer and are a treasure in themselves. The guided tours, conducted daily from May 30th through October 1st, provide a glimpse into the glittering past that is far removed from the cares of the present.

— Excerpts from the records of Evelyn Furman,
Owner of The Tabor Opera House

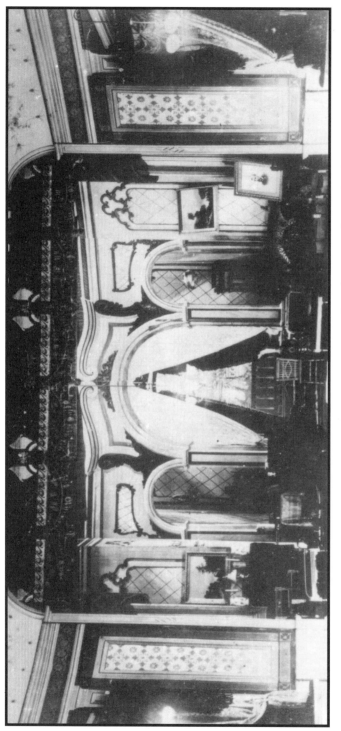

From the private collection of Evelyn Furman, The Tabor Opera House

Tabor Opera House

The stage of Tabor Opera House on opening night, November 20, 1879

Horace A. Tabor

Horace acquired the "Midas" touch. Although everything he bought made him richer, it did not bring him happiness.

Augusta L. Tabor

*Horace's first wife, Augusta, was not comfortable
with his new-found wealth.*

"Baby" Doe Tabor

"Baby" Doe was the third part of the "Tabor Triangle." She married wealth beyond her dreams — and died a pauper.

Courtesy of the Idaho Historical Society

Della Pringle

One of the best-loved Western entertainers

From the private collection of Evelyn Furman, Tabor Opera House
Photographer: Reutlinger, 21 Boulevard Montmartre, Paris, France

Anna Held

A Ziegfeld beauty and one of the loveliest entertainers

to visit the West

From the private collection of Evelyn Furman, Tabor Opera House

Maude Adams
America's first "Peter Pan"

Lillian Russell

*She represented all that was glamorous and
became the ideal of her generation.*

Nell Shipman

Chapter 4

TRAIL OF THE NORTH WIND

T
he golden era of the American theater slowly came to an end
during the early 1900s. With the arrival of the silver screen,
thousands of popular entertainers fell by the wayside as audiences eagerly rushed to view the marvel of moving pictures. Although
the first flickering two-reelers were crude, they fascinated the public
and the theaters were packed. New names began appearing on bill-
boards and marquees throughout the land. In 1921 Nell Shipman, a
pioneer both as a director in a male-dominated industry and a vocal
campaigner for animals, was added to the growing list of names.

Nell Shipman came into this world years before her time and
her story is as amazing as the woman herself. She was born in 1892
in British Columbia, Canada, and christened Helen Foster by her
parents, Arnold and Rose Barham. Shortly after her birth, the family
moved to Seattle, Washington where she grew up in a happy, uncom-
plicated home. Her parent's fondest dream was that of their lovely
daughter appearing on stage as a concert pianist. However, only half
of their dream came true — Nell did learn to play the piano, but she
was destined for greater heights than concerts. She discovered the
theater at the age of 12, and immediately lost her heart to the challenge and excitement of the stage.

At the early age of 13, Nell convinced her family to let her become part of Mr. and Mrs. Gilmore's touring company. The Gilmores
were a respected couple who guaranteed Nell's mother her child would
be well cared for and receive a theatrical education.

Nell, at 13, was a tall skinny outspoken girl and a quick study;
she could glance at a page and remember every word. By the time
the company left on tour, the young actress had landed the part of an

ingenue in one of their plays. It was quite a feat for one so young.

What started out as a lark, though, soon became a hard series of one night stands, lumpy beds in cheap hotel rooms and barely enough money for food. Nell learned to carry her belongings in an old trunk and to sit upon it when the sheriff came to attach the show's baggage for unpaid debts.

Also, during the tour, she saw the cruelty wild animals suffered at the hands of their trainers. Bobcats were shocked with electricity to make them snarl, and horses were thrown to the ground in pain when a wire was pulled taut so they would fall.

Nell was appalled at such treatment and would actively speak out against it. Years later, she wrote in her autobiography these words of a kind animal trainer, "We humans do not own animals, we borrow their companionship for a painfully short duration."

While with the Gilmores, Nell found she could act as well as survive in the tough entertainment world. At the age of 16, she moved up in her profession to leading lady in a play titled "The Girl From the Golden West." She was appearing under the name of Helen Barham at that time, and played a variety of roles.

In 1911, Nell married Ernie Shipman, a Shakespearean actor and manager of an exclusive chain of stock companies in the West; she was 18 years old and his fourth wife. Ernie fondly dubbed her with the pet name of Nell, and it was as Nell Shipman she gained fame. During her years with Ernie, Nell became a successful screen writer, director, producer and a star. The most important part of their marriage, however, was the birth of her son, Barry. Although he spent a great deal of his childhood with nurses and in and out of private schools, Barry and Nell shared a mutual devotion and respect for each other.

By 1915, moving pictures were becoming the fastest growing form of entertainment and the studios were expanding. Goldwyn was so impressed with Nell's acting ability and her skill in creating unusual screen plays, he offered her a seven-year contract. But, she turned him down to play the lead in Vitagraph's first full length wildlife adventure, "God's Country and the Woman." When the film was released she became known as a talented actress who knew her way around the outdoors. Her scenes with the wild animals were outstanding. Nell had a special way with them. She approached without fear and spoke in a soft, steady voice. They responded to her and performed without anyone inflicting pain.

Following the wildlife film, Ernie produced "Back to God's Country," with Nell playing the lead. The movie was shot on location in Canada, and broke box-office records with a 300 percent return for its investors. Nell became a household name and for the first time in years she had a few extra dollars.

While they were in Canada, Nell met Bert Van Tuyle, Ernie's production manager, and the two became very close friends. When the Shipmans returned to Hollywood, they mutually agreed to a divorce. As soon as the final papers were signed, Nell formed her own independent production company with Van Tuyle as her director. She became one of the few women who dared to compete in the male-dominated industry.

Nell's first movie, "A Bear, a Boy, and A Dog," starred her own cinnamon colored pet bear, Brownie, who weighed 200-pounds. The bear was a real ham with her unscheduled antics, and the delighted public wanted more. With that in mind, Nell elected to do what had never before been done. She decided to produce an action-packed, outdoor film that would be shot entirely on location in the wilderness titled, "The Grub-Stake." She didn't know the picture would be the beginning of a true-life melodrama, filled with incredible courage and deep, deep disappointment.

After careful consideration, Nell decided to do the indoor scenes of "Grub-Stake" at Minnehaha Studio in Spokane, Washington. She knew the owners and was familiar with the area. Her whole crew pitched in with the awesome move. They had to transport an entire zoo of over 200 wild animals from Hollywood, California, to Spokane, including Nell's own pets: Brownie, the bear; Laddie, a collie; Tex and his companion Lady, both malemutes; and Bobs and Babs, her bobcats. Bert Van Tuyle was in charge of production and Nell's son Barry would act in the film, when he wasn't attending school.

Nell was a whirlwind of activity. With her past success in wildlife films, and a lot of enthusiasm, she convinced several backers to help fund the venture. The money they put up helped pay for temporary quarters for the crew and animals, and established Nell as a producer.

When the Shipman Production Company arrived in Spokane, they were greeted with mixed emotions, as hundreds of cages of wild animals, boxcars of equipment, actors and the crew converged upon the city. It was a gigantic undertaking that few felt would succeed, but the lady herself had no doubts. Nell Shipman knew "The Grub-

Stake" would be the biggest and finest wildlife, silent film of all time.

The site at Minnehaha Studio was large and expensive, and the hotel bills for the crew and cast were astronomical. By the time they started filming, Nell claimed she was beginning to get "scared cold-silly inside." The indoor shots for the movie were done rapidly, as the crew consisted of experienced professionals. However, what had started out as a sure thing began to resemble a losing game. Newspaper reporters followed every move and referred to Nell as Mrs. Van Tyle (sic); her private life disappeared and was replaced with an almost empty bank account.

Nell and Van Tuyle had been combing the area for a perfect site to build their headquarters. When Nell first saw the splendor of Priest Lake, Idaho, she knew it was exactly what she wanted. The pristine lake, surrounded by treed forests and magnificent mountains, was the setting she had been seeking for her beloved animals and the wildlife films she intended to produce. Nell felt it was divine guidance that had led them there. Van Tuyle agreed, and the outdoor adventure that was to become news throughout America began.

Their temporary headquarters would be at Forest Lodge, a summer hotel at the mouth of the Thorofare, which connects upper and lower Priest Lake. The members of the company helped move all the wild animals and a vast amount of food and supplies to Coolin, Idaho by truck. From there everything was loaded on a large barge for the 21-mile trip to Forest Lodge, where they would remain for the winter.

Nell and Van Tuyle completed the outdoor shots for "Grub-Stake," at several sites, including Priest Lake, the Tiger/Ione area, and at Lake Heritage in Washington. After this complicated filming, necessitating several moves of actors, animals and equipment, the costly movie was finally ready.

With her animals cared for, Nell and Van Tuyle left in September, 1922 for Hollywood, thinking everything was under control. What they didn't consider was the weather. By December, the camp at Forest Lodge was below freezing and the lake solid ice. All supplies had to be brought in by sled from Coolin, at great expense, and Nell's company had to survive with a budget that was already strained. A few packed up and moved on and those who remained sat and waited with the animals.

When Nell finished editing "Grub-Stake," she and Van Tuyle traveled to New York to meet with the film magnates. She knew the success of the entire project depended upon Van Tuyle's business acumen and experience to consummate a lucrative financial deal. Unfortunately he became ill, and Nell had to go alone to sell her precious film to the highest bidder.

Although "Grub-Stake" appeared to be well-received, there weren't immediate offers to buy it. Nell felt that no one was interested and, being a novice as well as desperate, she accepted the first bid, which was very low. The next day Goldwyn was ready to sign a contract with her and would have paid a large advance. Since the rights had already been sold, Nell was left holding a nearly empty bag with a company and a zoo to maintain.

Nell and Van Tuyle left New York for Priest Lake with the money that had been raised, expecting to find her royalties from "Back to God's Country." The film, however, was having financial difficulties, so there was no check. Despite the setbacks, Nell returned to Priest Lake in high-spirits, loaded with food and supplies. She knew she was on the verge of bankruptcy but refused to admit it, even to herself.

In the spring of 1923, Nell began to build their permanent quarters at what was to be called Lionhead Lodge on Mosquito Bay, an isolated spot at the head of the lake. She had managed to obtain a 99-year lease on 103 acres of state land. Once again her company added their support and with the help of the locals, they built animal runs, shelters and primitive cabins with outdoor facilities. The whole scene took on the appearance of a great adventure with everyone laughing and cooperating. No one seemed to mind the kerosene lamps and that their only communication with the outside world would be by dog sled when the winter arrived.

With the camp ready, the animals were brought to their new home. At that time Nell owned the only camera-trained wild animal zoo in the country. With all the wilderness land that surrounded Lionhead, there was plenty of room to let them work in the open without leash or wires. During the day they were kept in camp by a circle of great danes, and safely locked in their cages at night. Nell also had her own pets and a dog team that consisted of 15 malemutes.

Nell had one huge problem, the never ending lack of funds. The winter supplies were so costly she began making personal appearances to promote "Grub-Stake," taking a few caged animals along for atmosphere. The larger cities advertised the film by painting dog paws along the sidewalks in front of their theaters. Although the movie was a success, all of the money she made went back into her company.

As winter set in, everyone became restless and bored. They had cabin-fever and were weary of the endless cleaning of the animal cages. The bills started to mount and Nell began producing small films shot in the snow, featuring stories of brave heroes and heroines fighting for survival. These movies contained spectacular nature scenes, and from them Nell's "Little Dramas of the Big Places" took root and grew. By keeping busy, the company managed to make it through their first winter.

The arrival of spring brought cheer to the entire crew. Nell was able to travel freely to promote "Grub-Stake" and produce her films. In July, she found out the boys of the Priest River Band needed uniforms, so she put on a benefit performance at the local theater and raised over $200. The band was so appreciative, they decided to visit the movie camp in person. Nell, always generous, had a large barbecue to entertain her neighbors, who came from miles around. The guests were greeted on the dock by Nell with Van Tuyle by her side and so the happy summer passed.

When the second winter arrived it was colder than the previous year. The bills were higher and money became very tight, the company was despondent. During these times Van Tuyle kept everyone going with his good nature. He had the ability to laugh at discomfort and was capable of doing almost anything, including fixing the broken down equipment. His constant smile elicited the admiration of the crew, and Nell referred to him as a "Top Banana," for she was beginning to draw from his strength.

As their funds dwindled down to almost nothing, Nell began doing all the cooking and camp washing. When the weather dipped well below freezing, Van Tuyle started complaining of a frostbitten right foot he had acquired while working in Canada; he was not his usual pleasant self. Things were rapidly falling apart. In order to bring in money, Nell wrote screen plays for Hollywood and traveled by dog sled across frozen land to show her small films at local theaters. The newspapers, who were following every move, began calling her the "Queen of the Dog Sleds."

Nell did everything she could to hold the company together, it was just one desperate attempt after another. She was like an old-time pioneer struggling for survival in the wilderness. The only difference was that most pioneers didn't have 200 wild animals to feed.

No one has recorded an accurate account of the nightmares Nell and her company endured that terrible winter. When the animal's food was about gone, she constructed a huge trough, and, with her arms bare to the elbows, Nell began mixing a combination of flour, cornmeal, bran and rye into hundreds of biscuits. With the game the men brought in, supplemented by berries and Nell's biscuits, the animals managed to survive. The crew was getting fed up with the weather and deprivation, and soon they began to leave one by one, creating more work for those who remained behind. Van Tuyle was in constant pain and irritable. When he saw Nell dancing with one of the few remaining actors, he accused her of having an affair and went to pieces. The actor left the next day and Nell tried to placate her partner.

The loss of Van Tuyle's good nature signaled the end of Shipman Production Company. Nell began to wonder about her own sanity. If his foot developed gangrene, what would she do, how would she get him to a hospital? These were questions she couldn't answer. Nell had scheduled a few personal appearances in hopes of picking up enough money to get them through what remained of the winter. The rest of the company had abandoned them by then, so she left Van Tuyle with a friend, and took off across the snow drifts in her sled. Her appearances, however, fell flat as one woman couldn't do a show all alone.

She returned to Lionhead filled with apprehension, and found Van Tuyle sitting in the dark rubbing his foot and moaning. The next morning he began wandering around in the snow looking for a way to leave. He had become a broken man filled with terrible pain. The worst part was his apparent hatred toward Nell. He would not let her get near him or touch him, and insisted upon taking a sled out alone. Although she knew Van Tuyle would not let her help him, Nell followed to be sure he didn't collapse and die in the snow.

The pair took off through the freezing weather, the man struggling with pain and the woman with anguish. When he could go no further, Nell managed to get him into her sled and took him to the edge of the lake. A friend helped put him in a boat for Coolin, where he could be transported to a hospital. Van Tuyle didn't lose his foot as Nell had feared, but he did lose several toes.

Nell, however, lost everything; no one could help her. She went down in a massive defeat with all she worked for gone. The animals were sold and shipped to a zoo in San Diego, California, including her own special pets. Lawsuits were filed; she was buried under a pile of debt. Her silent films though, went on to popularity.

Following the disaster, Nell said good-by to Van Tuyle, who was still distant toward her, and left for Hollywood. Somehow, she managed to pick up the pieces of her life and continued writing. The "Little Dramas" became known as "Little Dramas of the Big Places: Trail of the North Wind," and "Little Dramas of the Big Places: The Light on Lookout." Through the years critics have claimed Nell's films included some of the greatest outdoor scenes ever taken, and that the lady herself was one of outstanding courage.

Nell Shipman passed away in 1970, shortly after completing her autobiography, "The Silent Screen and My Talking Heart." She was a vital, dedicated woman who had no need to be liberated because she had already been born free.

Nell Shipman is regarded as a pioneer in the moving picture industry and listed in the "Silent Movie Hall of Fame." Her son, Barry Shipman, has over 70 television and moving picture credits and was part of the team that wrote series such as "The Lone Ranger," and "Dick Tracy." Nina Shipman Bremer, Nell's granddaughter, has appeared in feature length films. Both of her daughters, Westerly and Lani Beth, have made their film debut in moving pictures and television commercials. In 1977, the state of Idaho officially dedicated Shipman Point on Priest Lake and the "Idaho Film and Video Association" gives an annual Nell Shipman award. . .There has been a renewed interest in the Shipman films, and several can be found at the bookstore at Boise State University.

The author would like to thank the Special Collections Department at Boise State University, and Alan Virta, University Archivist, for providing the fine photographs of Nell Shipman and contributing much of the valuable information used in this chapter.

Shipman Zoo Animals Sure Of Eating

Since the story of the animals in the Nell Shipman zoo on Priest Lake being forced to go without food and in danger of dying was published last week, word comes from San Diego Park Zoo saying they want the animals and are willing to feed them and pay the cost of transportation to the California city.

This was the report Saturday from Harry Angstadt, owner of the Lone Star ranch on Priest Lake. Mr. Angstadt was up at the zoo last week and stated over the long distance telephone that there is now enough food there to run them for a week.

Saturday telegrams came from various parts of the United States offering aid for the animals, following the appearance of the story in papers throughout the country.

There was a great deal of excitement around the Great Northern depot Sunday when the Nell Shipman animals were loaded to be expressed to their new home in San Diego, California. The Priest Lake Transportation company brought the animals down from Coolin. They were loaded into a car and started on their journey Sunday afternoon. The three tons of animals included dogs, deer, bear, skunks, porcupine and various others, and in spite of reports to the effect that they had not been well fed, they were fat and in good condition when they left Priest River.

> — Northern Idaho News, Sandpoint June 16, 1925
> Courtesy of the Bonner County Historical Society

"The Grub-Stake" was filmed on location in the northwest.

Nell Shipman

As Faith Diggs in her production, "The Grub-Stake."

Forest Lodge at Priest Lake, Idaho

The lodge was the temporary headquarters for Nell Shipman's movie crew.

Nell Shipman

She brought the great Northwest to the world's movie screens.

Nell Shipman both starred and directed the silent movie "The Girl from God's Country." She played a duel role in the film which was quite demanding as she was constantly changing costumes and wigs. Although the picture was a success at the box office, it was a financial flop. Nell's talent, however, came shining through and she became one of the most popular stars of the silent film era.

Nell went on to star in "Back to God's Country," in 1919, and in 1922, she produced her own film, "The Grub-Stake," which established her as a writer, producer, director and star.

Nell Shipman
Vitagraph/Curwood Star, 1915-1920

Cowboy Jo was a Lady!

Chapter 5

THE HORSEMAN
WAS A LADY

E arly one morning in the 1850s, a stranger rode into Denver, Colorado, astride a small Missouri mule. He was dressed in worn, leather britches, wore a beat-up old Stetson and resembled a young boy with a watchful look in his eyes. The revolver and sheath knife on his hip left little doubt in anyone's mind that the lad could handle himself in any emergency ... And so begins the fascinating story of "Mountain Charley," who was either one, or two women, depending upon who is telling the strange tale.

During the days of the Wild West, it was not uncommon for a few daring women to cross the barrier and enter the male domain. However, most of these women had a reason to change their lifestyle. When Belle Starr was seduced by Cole Younger and learned to ride with his desperados, she couldn't return to the dignified life she had once led. Belle proved she could out-ride, out-shoot and out-wit most men, including those wearing a badge. Yet, she did it as a woman and attempted to retain her feminine attributes.

Calamity Jane, on the other hand, was more comfortable with men than women. She wore male attire, drove a team and cussed and drank like a sinner. But, Calamity never attempted to hide the fact that she was a woman. She always claimed, "I'm Calamity Jane and I sleep when and where I damn well please."

These two women adopted the male lifestyle head on as females, refusing to conform to the demands society imposed upon them. Other women like "Mountain Charley," "Little Jo (or Joe) Monaghan" and "Charley Parkhurst" couldn't stand up to the pressure of the Victorian era. They buckled under it, assuming the male persona because they felt it was the only way to increase their earning potential and live freely — things they could not do while retaining their role as women.

Rather than fight society, they discarded their petticoats and corsets and wore male attire, passing themselves off as men. Surprisingly, most of them actually enjoyed the transformation. Mountain Charley wrote in her autobiography, "I buried my sex in my heart and roughened the surface so I would not be discovered." As a man Charley could go where she chose and do as she pleased without breaking any rules. She was free to discover life and find work that paid a decent wage.

There are two versions of Mountain Charley's life. The more popular can be found in her autobiography, published by the University of Oklahoma in 1968. Her travels have also been documented in newspapers, and Horace Greeley, editor and politician, mentions her in his columns several times.

She was born Elsa Jane Forrest, of a rather clouded parentage, and raised by a kind man who claimed to be her uncle. Elsa ran away from her home at the age of 12 (she claimed to have been very mature) to marry her lover, a pilot on the Mississippi River. He was a fine man and good husband, who provided a home for Elsa and their two daughters. Although he was away most of the time, they lived a happy life until the night a stranger appeared at Elsa's door to inform her that a man named Jamieson had killed her husband.

Within weeks Elsa found herself penniless and homeless. Temporary relief was provided by the Masonic Lodge, but that would not last forever. She looked in vain for work that would supply enough income to support herself and her daughters. During her struggle for survival an intense hatred for Jamieson, the man who had killed her husband, began to grow and fester. Elsa knew she had to avenge her husband's death and support her children. To do both she would have to assume the identity of a man.

She tearfully placed her daughters in a home and went to a trusted friend of her husband for help. At first the man was shocked, as it was a very unusual request. He soon realized, however, that she had no other recourse and helped Elsa find masculine clothing that would fit her small frame. He further agreed to keep her secret and let her return to his home to change back to her own clothing when she visited her children. So, at the age of 16, Elsa became a duel personality.

In all outward appearances Elsa was a young man named

Charley. She already had a husky voice and the rest she learned by degrees. It took several weeks before Elsa was comfortable with her new role, but Charley finally emerged. She started working as a cabin boy for $35 a month. At first everyone wondered why the boy blushed when he heard obscene language, however, Charley soon learned to control that. She also learned to banish all her feminine traits and became a loner, avoiding any unnecessary conversation. At night Elsa emerged, haunted by the memories of her children and the death of her husband, and her hatred for Jamieson grew.

As time passed, Charley became more secure with the role of a man and began saving money. She visited her children every chance she could, in the form of Elsa. The friend was true to his word and Charley was able to come and go freely. Soon, she left her job as a cabin boy for better wages working for the railroad. That turned out to be a bad choice though, as Charley's superior suspected he was really a she. When the man invited the innocent Charley to accompany him and a friend to dinner, Charley overheard their lurid conversation about her being a woman, and hastily left. She returned to her room, packed her bags and boarded a steamer for Detroit.

Charley's new job was that of a brakeman on a train, and, to her surprise, Charley found a strange satisfaction in her new situation. She had acquired the tastes of the stronger sex and often walked about the town comfortably as a man. Charley mingled freely and traveled wherever she desired without fear, always stalking Jamieson.

During one of her walks, the inevitable happened, Charley came face to face with the dreadful man who had murdered her husband and she attempted to shoot him. Unfortunately the bullet missed and he wounded her. She managed to find refuge with a kind woman who listened to Charley's story and kept both her and her secret until Charley was well enough to travel. The incident frightened Charley so much she decided to leave the area and joined a company of men heading for the gold fields of the West. She was the only woman and no one suspected her sex.

Charley traveled on, saving her money and writing cheerful letters to her daughters. When she reached Sacramento, California, Charley accepted a job in a saloon and found she didn't mind the work; she actually enjoyed it. Her next venture was buying and selling mules, and it proved to be quite lucrative, for Charley ended up $2,500 ahead. She returned to what she referred to as the "States" where she spent as much time as possible with her children.

When Charley left on her next trip to California, she was at the head of a train of 15 men, 20 mules, horses and cattle. That trip netted her $30,000.

Charley's next venture was in Denver, where she opened a bakery and saloon. By that time she was known and respected as Mountain Charley, a mysterious young man who frequently traveled. While in Denver Charley finally found Jamieson, and this time she took careful aim. Her bullet found its mark, severely wounding the man. He died soon after, releasing Charley from the terrible revenge that had filled her heart. She was able to reveal her true identity to the world. Although Charley was free to become Elsa, she found she preferred to dress as a man and was comfortable with the name Mountain Charley.

She bought a saloon near Denver, and fell in love with her barkeeper, H.L. Guerin, who was aware of her past. Eventually Charley and Guerin were married and opened a boarding house. They sent for Charley's children and had a few of their own. In the eyes of the world, however, Elsa remained Mountain Charley, a strange woman who wore male attire the rest of her life.

In 1885, George West, publisher of the Golden Transcript, Golden, Colorado, shocked the West when he wrote a series of stories about "Mountain Charley," who he claimed was the least known woman of the Civil War. His revelations, however, were totally different from those in Elsa Jane Guerin's autobiography. West called the woman he met in 1860, "my strange little heroine," and told of becoming her friend and confidant. He said she only revealed her incredible story to him because he promised not to print it for 25 years. And, being a man of his word, West kept her life's experiences confidential for a quarter of a century before publishing them.

In his column West described her as a pretty boy about 22 years old. He said the small, mysterious person dressed as a male and frequently journeyed between Denver and the mountains. No one questioned her actions and most ignored her eccentricities, but all were curious about her past.

Although they often traveled together on the same stage, it was many months before Charley would trust West with her story. Even then she only granted him a personal interview because he saved her from an embarrassing situation. A group of young men suspected Charley was a woman, and to her horror they set out to have their way with her. West overheard her pleas for help and ran to the rescue. Years later, West wrote, "It was a thrilling, saddening narrative of young and trusting love, of sadness, desertion, and revenge."[1]

The woman told him she had been named Charlotte at birth and called "Charley" by her schoolmates. Her family lived on a small farm in Iowa, and they were very poor. When Charlotte was 18, her mother died leaving her with a stern stepfather who expected the girl to work, and discouraged any suitors who came her way. Charlotte knew very little about the outside world, so when a handsome man offered to take her away from the drudgery, she ran off with him.

The man did wed Charlotte and said he loved her, but it was not a happy marriage. He was a crooked gambler who treated her badly, then abandoned her for another woman. Charlotte's love turned to hatred and she began to plot revenge. Since it was a masculine world, she decided to carry out her plans as a man. Charlotte acquired male clothing, purchased a mule and headed West as Charley, for it was in that direction her husband had disappeared.

No one recognized or suspected Charley was a woman, and she struck out alone across the plains. The trail of her husband's dishonest deals was easy to follow and Charley found him; although she never reveals whether she actually killed him, it can be assumed she did. Once her revenge was fulfilled, Charley didn't care what happened to her life. She took things as they came, occasionally appearing as a woman, but more often as a man. After telling West her story, Charley disappeared from the area leaving him wondering where she was and what she was doing.

As tales of Mountain Charley grew, she began to shake up the male population with her deeds. The newspapers tore her reputation to pieces with stories that were usually not true. In late 1860, she was reportedly seen working as a bullwhacker in New Mexico, then drifted across the border to prospect for gold. One reporter said he saw her dealing faro in a Denver gambling house.

The next time West ran into Charley, however, was in the fall of 1864, during the Civil War. He was serving with his regiment in Missouri and on his way to see the general, when a small orderly appeared from out of nowhere. The young man approached carefully and in a soft voice whispered in West's ear that it was she, Charley. West could hardly conceal his astonishment when Charley laughed and said she was serving her country as an enlisted man named Charles Hatfield in the Iowa regiment. She told West she had been in the army two years and no one knew her sex.

[1]**Golden Transcript,** Jan. 14, 1885

During that period Charley said she had frequently acted as a spy for the Union Army and worked directly for Colonel Curtis. When it came time to part, Charley's last words to West were, "If we both live through tomorrow's fight, I'll see you again, friend George." And that was the last West heard of his little heroine until a letter arrived shortly after he wrote the first column about her life, 25 years later.[1]

After West read the letter and her enclosed diary, he was able to complete the story that had begun so many years before. Charley wrote that on the day of the great battle she received a bullet in one leg, a sabre slash across one shoulder and was left for dead. A confederate doctor was the first to find her and although he immediately discovered her sex, he did not reveal it to anyone. The following day the Union Army returned victorious, and Charley was placed under the care of another doctor who also kept her secret. She recovered fully, but would always have scars to remind her of the battle. Charley remained in the army until the end of the war and was mustered out as a first lieutenant.

When West finished the final column about Mountain Charley, he concluded with these words, "Upon her earnest solicitations, nothing more will be given of the life of the strange character after her return to civilian life...She is happily married, and with a tenderly loving husband and a family of loving children around her is in a sphere suited to her sex, loved and respected by all who know her ..."[2] So, who was the real Mountain Charley? Only the lady herself can tell —

Unlike Mountain Charley, Jo Monaghan's well-documented, touching story flows in a course as straight as her life. Jo didn't set out to avenge a husband's death, or fight in the Civil War, but in her own quiet way she was a true heroine of the West.

In the spring of 1868, a person who appeared to be a young man carefully guided his horse along the muddy, pockmarked main street of Ruby, Idaho. He was slim and graceful in the saddle and made every attempt to avoid the rough miners, cowpunchers and hard-eyed gun-slingers standing in the doorways. The newcomer was a little man, no more than five-feet tall in his high-heeled boots, and, in a community ruled by six-shooters, he was not packing a gun.

The men who lined the street silently watched as he swung out of his saddle, tied his horse to a hitching post and entered the hotel. While he was gone, the locals quickly gathered around his horse to see how far he had ridden, and it appeared he had come a long way.

[1]**Golden Transcript,** Jan. 14, 1885
[2]**ibid**

When the stranger emerged from the hotel, one of the men asked his name. With a tentative smile, the young rider, in a boyish voice replied, "Jo Monaghan, sir." Since few men were called sir in those days, the boy's politeness no doubt avoided any confrontations that might have erupted. The men looked at each other and then at the small tenderfoot, and they all wondered what he was doing in Ruby City.

Almost everyone in the West had a go at prospecting, and Jo was no exception. The little fellow purchased the necessary equipment and set out to dig for gold. A few weeks of hard labor, however, soon convinced him it was too much for his slight build. Although his hands were raw with blisters, Jo had stuck it out long enough to earn the respect of the community. Within a few weeks, the tough men of the rugged town began referring to him as "Little Jo," and it was obvious they accepted him in their frontier society.

When Jo realized he wasn't cut out to be a miner, he decided to become a sheepherder. The range was wide and the demand great for men who were willing to accept the lonely job — and Jo preferred to be alone.

He soon became a familiar sight with his carefully groomed horse, faithful dogs and hundreds of bleating sheep. Jo was out on the plains for months at a time without seeing another soul, but he never complained. For three years the little man lived an isolated life, carefully tending his flock and occasionally appearing in town. Then one day Jo realized he no longer needed the solitude; it was time to put the past behind and return to civilization.

Jo's next job was working in a livery stable, and in his usual competent way he earned the respect of the horsemen. One of them even offered to let him ride a wild bronco. When Jo accepted, the locals turned out in force to place a bet and watch their little friend get thrown. To the surprise of everyone, including himself, Jo managed to remain in the saddle. From then on there was no stopping him, and it was said there wasn't a horse that was too wild or savage for the gentle hands of Little Jo Monaghan—he became a legend. During the next year Jo learned to handle a lariat and mastered the use of both a rifle and pistol, becoming a sharpshooter.

No matter what he did or how hard he worked, however, Jo could never appear masculine. He just wasn't "one of the boys." Jo didn't smoke, cuss, drink alcohol or visit the "sporting houses." More than one said he was just "plumb not natural." He also preferred to sleep alone, rolled up in his blanket with only the stars for company; he never accepted the comfort and companionship of the bunkhouse.

The little fellow remained a mystery, but somehow people liked and accepted him. The only man he trusted though, was an elderly mining superintendent who he visited every week. Since Jo did not have any vices, he began placing his extra money in the hands of the superintendent to hold for him. The rest he faithfully mailed once a month to an address in the east.

Although Jo kept to himself most of the time for 15 years, he always managed to participate in his community. He attended the town-hall meetings and sat on a few juries. When it was time for an election, he was among the first to cast a vote.

In 1880, however, a tragedy struck that created an uproar for miles around. Jo's trusted friend, the superintendent, disappeared with all of his savings. A posse was quickly formed and the men combed the countryside for the thief. Unfortunately he made a successful escape and the money was never seen again. Little Jo's spirits were low for a brief period, but he soon perked up and decided he needed a change of scenery.

Jo left the mining area to homestead a piece of land on Succor Creek in Malheur County, Oregon. He built a cabin that has been described as a shelter of sorts, "haphazardly put together with the materials at hand ...Inside, a stout pole served as a bar across the door to keep out intruders when Jo's day's work was done."[1] It wasn't much, but the land and small cabin became a home the lonely man could call his own. He began raising a few livestock, and soon acquired a herd of cattle which were marked with his J.M. brand. Jo even had a friend, Fred Palmer, a farmer who lived a few miles away.

Palmer would always shout a few words of greeting when he passed the cabin, and the small man would drop whatever he was doing to return with a wave. One day in 1903, Palmer rode by the cabin and noticed there wasn't any smoke coming from the chimney and no one was in sight. He gave his customary greeting, but received no reply. Palmer went to the cabin and when he heard a racking cough from inside, he opened the door and found his friend near death. He carefully wrapped the little fellow in a blanket and carried him into town. Jo never regained consciousness.

The townspeople sent for the undertaker and gathered at the saloon to plan a suitable funeral. A few hours later, the door of the saloon burst open and the distraught undertaker came running in to

[1]**Owyhee Chronicle,** Homedale, Idaho, 1960

tell of the unbelievable, Little Jo Monaghan was a woman! Everyone was shocked and the whispers began. It seemed the mysterious little person had successfully pulled the wool over the eyes of the whole town.

A few trusted neighbors went to Jo's now empty cabin, and there, among her few belongings, was a little rusty trunk that contained her secret. They found a small bundle of old, well-read letters carefully wrapped in tissue. The letters were filled with love and revealed that Little Jo was really Josephine Monaghan, the once beautiful daughter of a wealthy family of Buffalo, New York.

Josephine had fallen in love with an older man who, after seducing her, would not accept his responsibilities. Ashamed to face her society parents, Josephine ran away to New York, where she gave birth to a baby boy. After a futile attempt to support the child, she left him with her sister to raise.

The desperate girl shed her feminine attire as well as her identity. She dressed as a young boy and headed West to make a new life for herself. The money Jo faithfully mailed East every month was to care for the son she would never again see.

Little Jo was laid to rest beside a creek near the cabin that had been her home for 20 years. The slight woman, who was raised to be a lady, paid a heavy price for her so called sin, that of loving a man too much and not very wisely.

Charlotte Darkey Parkhurst was the antithesis of Little Jo Monaghan. She was born around 1812 in New Hampshire, and placed in an orphanage while still an infant. Charlotte grew up in an atmosphere of poverty with a total lack of love. She learned from experience that life was far less complicated for men than women and, at the age of 15, she climbed over the wall to freedom dressed as a male.

Once on the outside, Charlotte adopted the name of Charles D. Parkhurst and set out to see what life had to offer a woman masquerading as a man. Since Charlotte had never known luxury, she did not expect more than her basic needs. She was used to hard work and although she was not tall, her body was strong and muscular.

Charlotte's first job was working in the stables of Ebenezer Blach, where she proved to be a diligent employee. The men admired her dedication and began calling her "Charley," a name that made the young girl feel at home. When her love of horses became evident, they taught her how to handle a team. Charley had an instinctive talent with animals, and her skill with the reins became quite proficient; she was soon considered one of the most popular drivers.

In 1850, Charley joined the thousands of men heading west to seek their fortune in the gold mines. Instead of prospecting for gold, however, Charley decided there was more money to be made in transporting it. Within a few months she became known as a stagecoach driver who didn't know the meaning of the word fear.

The early trails of California were no place for a lady — and no one ever accused Charley of being one. She chewed tobacco, smoked "two-bit" cigars and was known as one of the best "Whips" in the West. Her face was weathered by sun and wind, and brown tobacco stains, from the large chaw she always had in her cheek, could be seen on her chin.

Charley had a voice that was often described as a "whiskey tenor." Her shoulders had grown broad from the years spent holding the reins, and the pleated, blousy shirt she wore disguised any femininity she had left. Charley dressed in expensive trousers, a buffalo skin coat, fancy high-heeled boots and a broad Texas hat. Her small hands were covered with embroidered buckskin gloves, which were the only concession she made to being a woman. It was said they cost $20, and she never removed them, not even when she ate.

Some said she "cut a fancy figure," but never to her face. Charley could and would fight. She was strong enough to deliver a swift uppercut to the nose as well as any male, and if that didn't work Charley would use her long blacksnake whip. At 15 paces she could slice the end off an envelope or take a cigarette from the mouth of a man. In any barroom brawl, Charley was definitely the one a man wanted on his side. Later in life, when a horse kicked her in the eye, she was deprived of her sight on one side and began wearing a patch. She was given a new title, that of "One Eyed Charley."

Although Charley drove like she was "possessed," and would extend her horses to the limit, she had a feel for the road that brought her through safely. Her trips might have been hair-raising, but Charley never lacked for passengers. They appreciated her skill and clamored to sit in the special seat next to Charley and the six-shooter she always kept beside her.

With all of her masculine traits, Charley did not drink for fear of revealing her secret. At the end of a trip, she headed for the stables to sleep with her horses. She had learned to keep to herself and that meant sleeping alone. When the other "Jehu" (stagecoach drivers) kidded her about being aloof, Charley never failed to mutter that she liked horses better than people. And she did, for if anyone ever abused a horse around her, he was sorry for it.

One of Charley's greatest problems had to do with other women. She was known as a "Prince of the Ribbons," and the blushing ladies all admired "Silent Charley" as "he" sat upon "his" seat, dressed in "his" fancy attire. When the tittering women's admiration became unbearable, Charley would cuss the horses, spit tobacco and hit the curves. The passengers were usually sent flying in all directions, including the silly women whose hoop-skirts flew over their empty heads.

No doubt Charley was really having a good laugh at the stupid creatures. Needless to say, she never remained in one place for any length of time. Charley wasn't interested in having an affair with a woman and an affair with a man was out of the question. Her life was one of loneliness that continued to be so.

For all her gruffness, however, Parkhurst cared about others. She helped women in need, assisted in childbirth and donated money to underprivileged children, especially orphans. Charley always carried candy in her pocket beside her chaw of tobacco. If a youngster became cross or frightened while riding in her stage, she would pull out a sweet. The smile that filled a little face never failed to bring a happy twinkle to Charley's one remaining eye.

Although Charley could run both wheels of her stage over a quarter laying in the road, with her horses galloping at full speed, she never boasted of her skills. The other whips spoke for her, describing Charley as an expert driver who understood "his" business and was a pleasant, steady "feller."

When the gold rush ended, Charley retired to Soquel, California, where she raised cattle and farmed a piece of land. She became a pillar of the community and an active member of the Odd Fellows. Charley believed every citizen had the right and the obligation to vote, and on November 3, 1868, at the age of 57, Charles D. Parkhurst, farmer, cast "his" vote in the National Election. Charlotte was the first woman in the United States, known to have voted in a national election, 52 years before the passing of the 19th amendment — only she had to vote as a man.

In 1879, Charley became ill with a persistent sore throat. Being Charley, she treated herself as she did her horses, with patent remedies. Her ailment became worse, and when she finally saw a doctor

Charley found she had cancer of the throat and tongue. All those days of chewing tobacco and smoking cigars had left their toll. She died a few weeks later.

Her secret was discovered while she was being prepared for burial. They found Charley was a well-endowed woman who at one time had had a baby, though nobody knows when. Her best friend was mortified and greeted her death with a few choice oaths, and the community was shocked. Regardless of her sex, Charlotte "Charley" Parkhurst was one of the most skilled and famous Whips in the exciting days of the gold rush, and as such she deserves to be remembered.

Charley Parkhurst, Jo Monaghan and Mountain Charley were all unusual women who chose to live their lives as men. They did it their way, without harming anyone, and each in her own way left a mark in the turbulent history of the Old Wild West.

Cowboy Jo Was A Woman
American-Journal Examiner, Great Briton, 1904

"Albeit, the life of 'Little Jo,' the recluse was admittedly a pure one and above all suspicion, it must be confessed that he was an object of much consideration and attention from the countryside. His pronounced feminine appearance, the boy's voice, his delicate build, the ascetic life he lived, all tended to bring his life under discussion. But never did anyone give utterance to the belief that he was anything other than the man he represented himself to be. And not until death had its clammy finger on him was the secret of this disguise penetrated. . .

After the discovery of the identity of her sex the neighbors of Succor Creek took the body out to the banks of the small stream and buried it. It was a heartrending sight. Not a word was spoken, not a word read, nor a prayer offered as the souless tabernacle of the once beautiful girl was laid to rest in the bosom of Mother Earth. . . The property that Jo left has been taken in charge by Fred Palmer. of Jordan Valley, who will hold it until the living relatives of the lonely woman man put in a claim for it or it becomes forfeited to the county legally by lapse of time."

— Courtesy of the Denver Public Library

---

from the Pajoronian, October 3, 1917 (Watsonville, CA)

Ben Holliday, the moving spirit in the Overland Stage Line, had to hire new drivers every Monday. The perils of the steep mountain grades where the horses hooves cut groves into the banks on either side thinned out his drivers fast. The following was recorded during one of his interviews:

There were, perhaps, fifty applicants for the positions: "'Ever drive a stage; how long? How near could you drive to the edge of a bluff with a sheer drop of a thousand feet with perfect safety to yourself, team and passengers.' Finally, one more than the rest, was willing to take a chance in driving with one-half of the tire over the cliff. About this time our Charley's turn came around. After putting in between his jaws, a fresh chew, he closed his jack-knife. . .He had gotten nearly to the door before he finished his answer: 'No, I won't suit you Mr. Holliday, for I would keep as far from that cliff as the mule would let me.' 'Yes? Well you take this slip into that room and tell the clerk to send you out by the first coach. . .'"

— Courtesy of the Watsonville Public Library

Josephine went from society debutante
to the guise of "Cowboy Jo"

The Jehu

"The fearless and sure Jehu safely guides the highest nettled horses, those untamed broncos of a Spanish sire and dam, with the lives of sometimes 19 passengers resting easily in the palm of his clenched hand, the flick of his whip, or the multiple reins. No matter how stormy the night, how long, dark or dreary, he seldom fails in his judgement or skill. How many errands he handles on the stage road; parcels purchased and carried, from cambric needle to grindstone. And the treasure he carries, bills he pays, and how honestly. Bank presidents, brokers and men in high stations may embezzle, but not the Prince of the Ribbons. He is not overpaid for all this, but he had one consolation. There is none so high, none so rich, none so profane, none so religious, none so poorly dressed or richly clad, but they all want to sit alongside the driver.

"Presidents, priests, editors, judges, Senators, my ladies with the golden tresses and rich laces, all are troubled with the same weakness: 'Agent, give me a seat alongside the driver.'"

— Article by one C. C. Bush, 9/5/1878
Courtesy of The El Dorado Historical Museum

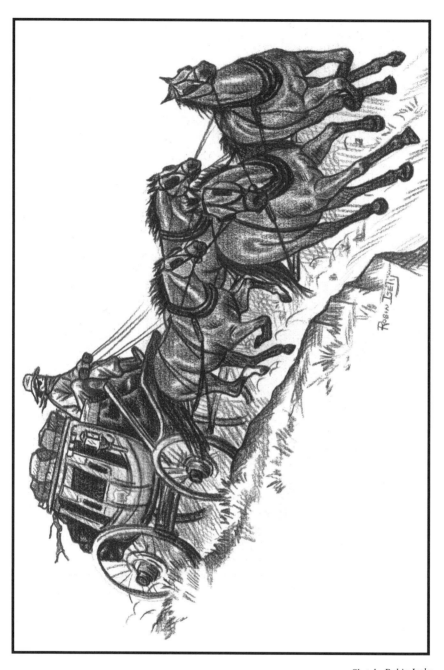

Sketch: Robin Isely

"Charley!"

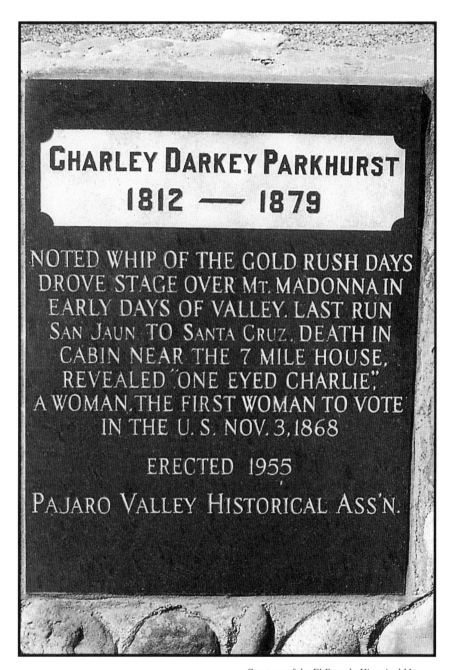

CHARLEY DARKEY PARKHURST
1812 — 1879

NOTED WHIP OF THE GOLD RUSH DAYS
DROVE STAGE OVER Mt. MADONNA IN
EARLY DAYS OF VALLEY. LAST RUN
SAN JAUN TO SANTA CRUZ. DEATH IN
CABIN NEAR THE 7 MILE HOUSE,
REVEALED "ONE EYED CHARLIE",
A WOMAN. THE FIRST WOMAN TO VOTE
IN THE U. S. NOV. 3, 1868

ERECTED 1955

PAJARO VALLEY HISTORICAL ASS'N.

Courtesy of the El Dorado Historical Museum

Charley's Monument

Delia Haskett

Delia drove the Wells Fargo stage over the treacher-
ous trails of early California from 1876 until 1885.

Chapter 6

THOSE WELLS FARGO WOMEN

O ne of the most welcome sights on the American frontier was that of the Wells Fargo stage, bouncing along over the rocky roads. To the pioneers, it meant a bit of civilization had arrived, and the whole community usually turned out to check the cargo. Most of the townspeople were anticipating a letter from home, others valuables, and a few awaited the arrival of a loved one. When the stage driver reached his destination and stepped down from the coach, he received a warm welcome, becoming the hero of the hour. Although it has been assumed all Wells Fargo stage drivers were men, that wasn't necessarily so, at least in California.

From 1876 to 1885, a beautiful young woman was the relief driver for the Lakeport - Ukiah run. Delia Haskett drove her stage over the dangerous Cow Mountain Range, past the deep, mysterious Blue Lakes, in to Upper Lake, through the sparsely settled Scotts Valley and on to Lakeport. The ride was a distance of about 45 miles, which on a good trip took approximately eight hours; the fare was $3.00, one way.

Delia was a true daughter of the West, born in Potter Valley, California in 1861. Her parents, Miranda, a teacher, and Samuel Haskett, the Wells Fargo agent in Ukiah, California were early pioneers.

As a tiny girl, Delia became fascinated with stagecoaches and began riding with her father before her feet could reach the floorboard. She constantly begged for the "ribbons" (reins), and her indulgent father let her have them whenever possible.

Little by little, the girl became more proficient. By the time she was 14, Delia was capable of taking the smaller runs and was trusted with the valuable mail. When one of the regular drivers was suddenly taken ill, she volunteered to take his place. Since Delia was the only one available her father let her go, and her career with Wells Fargo began.

As the girl pulled out with the coach, the postmaster warned her to watch out for road agents, as a band of highwaymen had been reported in the vicinity. Delia knew the route well, but she had two fears. The first was one all Wells Fargo drivers shared; they were constantly on guard for Black Bart, the notorious stage robber. Her other fear was safely passing the treacherous Blue Lakes in Lake County. The lakes were so deep and dark that even the local Pomo Indians refused to go near them. They claimed there was a monster lurking beneath the mysterious waters.

Delia left late in the evening and there were no passengers on that trip. She cracked her whip, urging the horses on past the shadowy trees that passed by on each side of the coach. The road was barely a trail and in some areas she let the horses have the lead, knowing they could follow the route far better than any human.

Around 11 p.m., when Delia pulled off the road to let the horses drink at a stream, she heard the clatter of hooves and the voices of many men coming her way. Delia's heart began to pound. She thought of finding a place to hide, but decided to sit and wait. When the noisy group came closer, she realized they were singing religious songs! The men soon surrounded the girl and she found her fears were groundless, it wasn't Black Bart after all; merely a group of singers returning from a religious camp meeting. At 3:00 a.m. the next morning Delia pulled up in front of the Wells Fargo office in Lakeport, tired but successful.

For the next nine years Delia drove the stage whenever she was needed. She became the first woman stage driver on record to carry the U.S. mail in California and the only female in the Pioneer Stage Drivers of California Association.

During her years with Wells Fargo, Delia became a crack shot with a long barreled pistol and could hit a nickel in mid-air. She was also an expert with the whip. Delia, however, did more than drive a stage. She rode in horse races, performed trick riding exhibitions and won prizes for her shooting skills. When she became Mrs. Rawson in 1885, Delia left her stagecoach days behind, and with her husband went on to become part owner in a mine, lady rancher and businesswoman. She never forgot her earlier days though, rattling along in the stage, cracking her whip and braving the dangerous California trails.

On September 21, 1906, the *Ukiah Republican Press* printed this news article: "Mrs. Delia B. Rawson, who will be remembered as Miss Delia Hasket (sic) formerly of this city, and now one of the leading business women of Los Angeles, is the recipient of a write up in the National Visitor of Los Angeles of a recent date. Mrs. Rawson is one of the most successful business women of the south and through her good business judgement has acquired a fortune. Her many old friends in this city are pleased to hear of her success."

Although it has been said that "Charley" Parkhurst also drove a Wells Fargo stage, she is not recognized as one of their drivers. A popular story of the gold rush tells of Charley being robbed by a bandit, and ordered to throw down the "box." It is believed to have been a Wells Fargo box that contained gold. From that day on Charley always carried a six-shooter by her side. The next time she heard someone repeat the same command, she grabbed the gun and killed an infamous highwayman. No one knows how many women drove a stage during the mid-1800s, but no doubt there were more than a few. The records of that day were poorly chronicled, so who can really say?

Hank Monk, legendary stagecoach driver, was a pal of Charley's and drove for Wells Fargo. One day Monk gave Horace Greeley the ride of his life from Lake Tahoe, down the mountains of the Sierra into Placerville, California, and got him there "on time," but a bit shaken. Monk was a hard-driving man with a large capacity for alcohol and like Charley, he had the courage to take a stage over roads that were barely trails. Levi Strauss, while riding with him in 1872, noticed his corduroy attire which was patched with copper rivets. The rivets held the material together so well, Strauss adopted the method, and the idea for the famous "Levi's" that we wear today was born.

Holding up the stage was a common occurence in the early West, and Wells Fargo carried most of the gold, silver and money in the mining areas. Between 1870 and 1884, they had 347 robbery attempts and the company began hiring "shotgun messengers." Wyatt and Morgan Earp were among the men who guarded the valuable shipments. If a bandit managed a successful holdup, Wells Fargo had skilled detectives to hunt him down, and they seldom failed to get their man.

Black Bart, one of the most notorious highwaymen, was the plague of Wells Fargo, as he robbed only them. During 1875 and 1883, he worked the lonely roads of California, and successfully held up 27 stagecoaches in 28 attempts. Bart was a slender man with brown hair and brilliant blue eyes, who always wore a flower in his lapel and left a poem taunting the company. He resembled a distinguished businessman, and by talking to the drivers, found out when a stage carrying valuables was scheduled to leave. Once he obtained the information, Bart would put on a derby hat, cover his face with a sack and hide in the bushes waiting for the stage.

In 1883, Bart robbed his last stage near Sonora, California. He stepped out from the bushes with his shotgun in his hand and ordered the driver to give him the box. Bart got the money, but when the driver started shooting he fled, leaving a handkerchief and his hat. The handkerchief had a laundry mark "F.X.O.7," and James B. Hulme, a Wells Fargo detective, traced it to San Francisco and arrested the "villian."

Oddly enough, the infamous Black Bart, who struck terror into the hearts of so many drivers, was merely an innocent looking, mild mannered man. He was a supposedly respectable mining engineer named Charles Boles. Black Bart was sent to San Quentin Prison for four years, and upon his release in 1888, was never seen again.

The name Wells Fargo always brings to mind the days when the West was young, filled with rugged cowboys, shoot-outs and stagecoaches. Both the West and Wells Fargo, however, offered more than violence. Thousands of respectable agents represented the company thoughout the United States, and, listed among the names are those of a few California women.

Each individual agent was issued a Wells Fargo certificate, specifying the duties and acknowledging his or her appointment. The men and the women were responsible for forwarding and receiving packages of all kinds, including gold dust and drafts for large amounts of money. The agents had to be honest, reliable, accurate, and in many cases, brave. "Wells Fargo agents nearest to the scene of a holdup coordinated the pursuit of the outlaws. One such agent was Cassie Hill at Roseville, California, from 1884 to 1908. She also represented Western Union Telegraph and the Southern Pacific Railroad." [1]

Most of the agents operated their own business as well as the Wells Fargo office. The following women were California agents:

[1] **Wells Fargo since 1852,** Wells Fargo and Company, 1988

In Mariposa, sisters Julia Jones and Lucy Miller alternated the job as agent from 1885 to 1909. Julia, a school superintendent and Lucy, a postmistress, were also actively involved with the affairs of their community; Mattie Bates, the agent at Corning, from 1890 to 1893, was also the local telegraph operator; in Navarro, Jennie Severance was the agent from 1896 to 1900, and also helped her husband run their hotel; Marie Devine, the Sierra City agent from 1899 to 1906, was not married while working for Wells Fargo, her only job.

Marie had several interesting experiences during her seven years as an agent. She was not only a respected member of society, but a heroine. One night in 1903, Marie worked late into the evening, and it was close to 8:00 p.m. when she left for home. As she approached the river near her house, she heard a plea for help and found a man almost frozen to death. Marie hurried back to town through the heavy snow, sounded the alarm, and led the rescue team to the scene. Later, *The Mountain Messenger* wrote, "His clothes were frozen and had to be cut off of him. After a couple of hours of rubbing and chafing him he was brought to his normal condition. He can thank his lucky star that Miss Devine heard his cries and gave the alarm."

The mountainous roads into Sierra City were dangerous and often a stage would go off the edge, into a tree, or overturn. Whenever a stage was damaged, Marie had to go to the site of the accident and check the cargo. Everything had to be accounted for, it was the Wells Fargo way, and she was a very capable lady.

When Marie married in 1906, she left her position with Wells Fargo and no one was named as her replacement. The era of the automobile had arrived and the days of the stagecoach were numbered. Those wonderful women of Wells Fargo, however, left their mark in the communities of the West and were sorely missed.

During their years as agents, these women took care of a diverse cargo, as Wells Fargo would carry almost everything. Live animals were shipped by express only, so they could be watered and fed. At one time a camel was loaded aboard for a circus. Monkeys, kangaroos, Philippine water buffalos and often a mad lion or bear, which would frighten the nervous express messenger, provided a bit of excitement. Once a setting hen was added to the cargo with the appropriate warning, "Setting hen—eggs expected to hatch. Handle with care." Practically anything was shipped, except skunks or volatile substances.

There were also lively ladies in fashionable gowns, rich gentlemen with top hats and canes, small children, the sick or injured, and even dead bodies. All were well cared for and delivered safely. No matter what the cargo, the Wells Fargo women handled everything that came their way with competence and integrity.

The wives of the Wells Fargo agents often worked beside their husbands; it was a demanding, responsible position. In 1852, one agent described the operation of his large express office and banking house in Auburn. "What I have to do is quite confining—staying in my office all day until 10 at night buying dust, forwarding and receiving packages of every kind, from and to everywhere, filling out drafts for the Eastern Malls in all sorts of sums..."[1] Another wrote, "Were it not for this feeling of resposibility and trust, I would be as light hearted as a bird."[2] It would appear a wife would be very handy to have around.

In 1854, William Daegener became the Wells Fargo agent in Columbia, California. He was a well-educated man from Germany and known throughout the county as an upright, progressive businessman. Before leaving Germany, Daegener had become betrothed to 20 year-old Maria Schultz. She was a strong German woman, who would be a fine wife and partner.

Maria left for the United States in 1855, and, following a long journey by ship, river-steamer, foot portage and mule-back, she arrived in San Francisco. Three days later she and William Daegener were married and set off for Columbia, filled with optimism.

The new bride liked everything about the community and immediately set to work fixing her home, which was above the Wells Fargo office. Each morning she came down to help her husband, freeing him to go about whatever needed attending. The customers liked her cheery personality and the locals would stop by to just say hello. Maria was made to order for her role as the wife of a Wells Fargo agent.

William Daegener became increasingly successful in his business affairs and in 1856 he was able to buy the American Hotel, in which the company was located. When fire destroyed the structure in 1857, he saved the Wells Fargo records and started building a new agency.

Maria helped both socially and physically whenever she was able, for within a few years the Daegener family had become a large one. Their living quarters were spacious and always filled with guests. Both locals and travellers were always welcome at the agent's home;

[1]**Wells Fargo since 1852**, Wells Fargo and Company, 1988
[2]**ibid**

Maria was a friendly women who enjoyed entertaining. Daegener would often receive letters from San Francisco business acquaintances that usually concluded with, "Pray present my respects to your good lady with thanks for her hospitality."

The Daegeners were successful and happy. William was a man of affairs as well as a leading member of his community—Maria was his chief asset. Unfortunately, money couldn't buy health. Three of their five children died within a week from a scarlet fever epidemic that ravaged Columbia in December, 1862. The Daegeners buried them in the hilltop cemetery near the school. Their other two children were also very ill, so Maria decided to take them back to Germany for better medical attention.

She left Columbia in the spring, amidst the well-wishes of their friends and neighbors. The doctors in Germany though, proved no better than those in the United States, for another daughter died, leaving Maria and William with only one daughter, five-year-old-Louise.

In 1872, the family left Columbia, as William Daegener gave up the Wells Fargo agency and sold all his holdings. They moved to Napa Valley, California and things went well for the family until Daegener was thrown from his buggy, losing his hearing. The family returned to San Francisco, where they lived the rest of their lives.

The Daegeners are remembered for being an integral part of the frontier during the days when California was young. The old Wells Fargo building where they lived and worked still stands in what is now Columbia State Park. It represents a symbol that was once recognized throughout the world, that of a stagecoach pulled by six horses. A sign on the faded wall welcomes visitors with these words, "Pay no more for dust than it is worth, nor pay less"....A fitting motto for the thousands of hardworking men and women who won the trust of their community as well as the respect of the West.

Tips for Stagecoach Travelers

The best seat inside a stage is the one next to the driver. Even if you have a tendency to sea-sickness when riding backwards you'll get over it and will get less jolts and jostling. Don't let any "sly elph" trade you his mid-seat.

In cold weather don't ride with tight-fitting boots, shoes, or gloves. When the driver asks you to get off and walk do so without grumbling, he won't request it unless absolutely necessary. If the team runs away. . . sit still and take your chances. If you jump, nine out of ten times you will get hurt. In very cold weather abstain entirely from liquor when on the road, because you will freeze twice as quickly when under its influence.

Don't growl at the food received at the station. . . stage companies generally provide the best they can get.

Don't keep the stage waiting. Don't smoke a strong pipe inside the coach. Spit on the leeward side. If you have anything to drink in a bottle pass it around. Procure your stimulants before starting, as "ranch" (stage depot) whiskey is not "Nectar."

Don't lean or lop over neighbors when sleeping. Take small change to pay expenses. Never shoot on the road, as the noise might frighten the horses. Don't discuss politics or religion.

Don't point out where murders have been committed, especially if there are woman passengers.

Don't lag at the washbasin. Don't grease your hair, because travel is dusty. Don't imagine for a moment that you are going on a picnic. Expect annoyances, discomfort, and some hardships.

— Omaha Herald, 1877

Courtesy of the El Dorado Historical Museum, Placerville, CA

Black Bart

Black Bart, the notorious highwayman, terrorized the lonely stagecoach roads of California from 1873 to 1884.

Lucy Miller

Lucy was the Wells Fargo agent in Mariposa, CA, from 1885 to 1892, and from 1902 to 1909. When she became postmistress, Lucy moved the mail service into the Wells Fargo office.

Julia Jones

Julia, a school superintendent, alternated the position of Wells Fargo agent in Mariposa with her sister, Lucy. Julia was the agent from 1892 until 1902.

Courtesy of Columbia State Park, Columbia, CA

Wells Fargo's Columbia office during the 1870s

The old building is still standing today.

Maria Daegener

Maria was the wife of William Daegener,
Columbia's Wells Fargo agent from 1854 to 1872.

A concord stagecoach in the early 1870s carrying passengers, mail and Wells Fargo Express in northern California.

Wells Fargo Trivia

The precious little "box" that was the treasure the highwaymen sought, rested in the front "boot" of a Wells Fargo stagecoach, beneath the drivers feet. It weighed 24 pounds, measured 20 x 12 x 10 inches, and was built of Ponderosa pine, reinforced with oak rims and iron straps and corners. The words "Throw down the box," shouted by a masked man holding a gun, always struck fear into the heart of the driver, male or female.

Julia Bulette, the notorious red-light lady of Virginia City, Nevada, lived and worked in her cottage at the corner of Union and D Streets. It was the most elaborate "house" on the "row." The parlor could accommodate as many as a dozen visitors and the furnishings were plush. Julia, however, added a real touch of class when she had fresh flowers delivered daily from San Francisco, via Wells Fargo — or so the story goes!

In 1864, many felt Adah Isaacs Menken was an odd lady for riding into Virginia City, Nevada, on the front seat of the Wells Fargo stage with her back to the horses. There was nothing strange about it though, as Adah was busy watching the stage behind, which was carrying the stallion for her performance of the "Mezeppa." Wells Fargo hauled almost everything in that day, and the lady was merely watching over her horse.

During the mid-1800s, the arrival of a ship in San Francisco, was announced by a semaphore, accompanied by noisy bells, whistles and often a brass band. A ship meant mail and messages from loved ones left behind. Large lines immediately formed at both the U.S. post office, and, of course, Wells Fargo, for everyone knew within minutes, some of the precious cargo would be in the capable hands of the agent.

Mary Richardson Walker
Missionary

Chapter 7

SCHOOLMARMS
WITH A CAUSE

I n the early 1830s, a young woman named Mary Richardson was attending the Maine Wesleyan Seminary when she asked her professor how her papers compared with those the young men handed in. He replied, "They are much better. Aren't you ashamed?"

This was the educational atmosphere for a young woman of that era. She was permitted to attend a class but she could not take an examination or gain credit for her work. Females were expected to be dependent upon their husbands or male relations; to function independently was unthinkable — and many intelligent women joined the westward movement as schoolmarms in search of adventure and freedom.

Although the 19th century stereotype of a schoolteacher was that of an angular spinster or a prim and proper young miss, in reality she was neither of the above. Many of these ladies came from influential eastern families, a few were filled with burning ambition and others were seeking a better life or a husband. All, however, were dedicated to their profession. Despite low wages, overwork and primitive, uninviting schoolrooms, these women brought a degree of morality and education to the raw communities. A few of the schoolmarms became missionaries, others suffragettes and one went on to become the first woman to hold office in the United States House of Representatives.

Mary Richardson Walker, one of the earliest schoolmarms, was a woman of great vision who gave up her personal freedom to become a missionary. During her lifetime, she experienced few moments of satisfaction and many hours of despair.

Mary was born on the Richardson's farm in 1811. Her mother was a gentle woman who was content to follow Mary's father, a man poor in worldly goods, but rich in education. The Richardson family was one of close-knit, pious individuals who were devoted to each other. Their home was filled with books and the children were allowed to make their own decisions. Since Mary was the eldest of the nine Richardson offspring, she assumed the duties of the household chores, cooking and cleaning for the family. Often, while she worked, the young girl dreamed of traveling to far away places where she could teach sinners the words of God. She knew she was meant for better things than the drudgery of housework, dressing birds and cleaning tripe, a job she found loathsome.

At the age of 19, Mary entered the Wesleyan Seminary where she pursued one of the few careers open to women of the 19th Century, teaching. Mary was an attractive girl who possessed a good sense of humor and excellent health. She did not suffer from a lack of admirers and in a letter to one of her brothers, she wrote: "There are beaus that want to call on me full often as I want to see them. In a place like this, I would give more for one brother than all so many beaus."[1] At times, Mary worried because she couldn't seem to please everybody and that she wouldn't find a man perfect enough to please her.

In 1833, when Mary was 22, she began teaching school and found it brought her great pleasure. She soon began to teach Sunday school also. Mary was filled with vitality and happy with her life. Occasionally, however, dark thoughts would cross her mind. She knew she was growing older and felt if she didn't get married soon she wouldn't be able to find a good man at all!

Eventually, Mary decided to fulfill her dreams of becoming a missionary. But, when she applied to the American Missionary Board, she found a lone woman was not acceptable. Mary didn't know that a young man named Elkanah Walker was also seeking a post as a missionary. This man was informed he should have a "good" wife before he could be considered

Elkanah was an over zealous Christian who opposed anything frivolous, including dancing. He was shy, sedate, above "wickedness" and wanted an honorable woman who would do his bidding. When the missionary board turned him down, Elkanah also became concerned about marriage. Mary needed a husband and Elkanah a wife. With the aid of the board and a mutual friend, they finally met.

[1] **Mary Richardson Walker: Her life**, by Ruth Karr McKee, 1945

It was not love at first sight, but the diminutive Mary felt she could learn to love the tall, dark-haired, religious man.

On March 5, 1838, when Mary was 27 years-old, she married Elkanah Walker. Her wedding dress was black, as befitted a missionary's wife. Later she wrote in her diary, "The name Walker seems to me to imply a severed branch. Such I feel myself to be."[1] Elkanah referred to Mary as Wife or Mrs. Walker.

Following the wedding, the couple left for old Oregon. As the Walker's wagon disappeared from sight, one of the Richardson family friends remarked: "That is just like Mary Richardson to go galloping off across the plains on a wild buffalo."[2] So began Mary's life as a wife and mother, and, unfulfilled missionary.

The Walkers traveled with another newly married couple, Cushing and Myra Eells, who were also missionaries. The trip was long and hard, especially for Elkanah, as he was ill and depressed most of the time. Elkanah appeared to be constantly upset with Mary. When she revealed to him she was ambitious, he recommended she read the Bible or a good book of female education in order to become a worthy prize for her husband.

Elkanah also resented traveling on the Sabbath and Mary began to question her own faith during those times — everything in her life seemed to be a failure. She couldn't please her husband and was afraid Christianity would also become a delusion.

Six months later and three-thousand miles from home, the Walkers and the Eells joined Dr. and Mrs. Whitman at the Oregon Country mission at Waiilatpu, near Walla Walla. While their station between Colville and Spokane was being built, the two women remained with the Whitmans. The new station, called Tshimakain, was situated in a lovely spot among the Spokane Indians. Six of Mary's eight children were born there, and she learned that life in the west was far more complicated than life in Maine. There was constant work to be done and her one-room hut had only an open hearth to cook upon.

The Walkers and the Eells decided the best way to instruct the Spokanes was to help them to learn English. As a former schoolteacher, Mary created hymns for them to sing. She soon realized, however, that she was not to teach as she had planned. There was too much work to do. Elkanah was away most of the time and he often frowned upon his wife's attempts to educate.

Mary found herself the center of attention as the Indians con-

[1]**Women's Voices from the Western Frontier,** by Susan G. Butruille, 1995
[2]**First White Woman Over the Rockies**, by Clifford Merrill Drury, 1963

stantly observed her, and attempted to imitate her ways. In this manner, she found that although there were no classes, she could teach the art of sewing, cooking and making soap, for the Spokanes displayed a great desire to bathe. They were also fond of music and learned to sing sacred songs instead of the "profane" French ditties they had picked up from the fur traders.

As the children kept arriving, Mary learned to attend to her own birthing. She wrote in her diary: "Rose about five. Had early breakfast. Got my housework done by nine. Baked six loaves of bread. Made a kettle of mush now have a suet pudding and beef boiling . . . May the merciful be with me through the unexpected scene. Nine o'clock p.m. was delivered of another son."[1]

The life of Mary Walker continued on in this manner until the tragic Whitman massacre of 1848. Mary was 37 years-old when the family was forced to abandon both their home and Tshimakain. She had borne six children while at the mission and now she was forced to leave all she owned behind. The work she had dreamed of had not been accomplished and Mary realized she was only a wife and mother, not a missionary. The Spokane Indians watched over Tshimakain for many years, singing their hymns and waiting for their missionary friends who never returned.

Elkanah eventually settled his family in Forest Grove, Oregon, and Mary had to learn to cook all over again, for she had never used a stove. Elkanah, in poor health and disillusioned, left the small farm he had acquired to minister to the surrounding churches. Mary continued to work for education and helped with the fundraising to build an academy in Forest Grove. She sold her own gold watch to add to the building fund.

With Elkanah gone most of the time, Mary raised her children alone, assuming the responsibilities without a word of reproach to her husband. She remembered the days so long ago when she knew she was destined for nobler things. In her diary Mary wrote: "Life seems to me a weary task and every year brings it nearer to its completion."[2]

In 1897, at the age of 86, Mary Richardson Walker passed away — her life had ceased years before when all her dreams disappeared and her memory began to fade. In 1945, her granddaughter, Ruth Karr McKee, carefully edited Mary's letters and diaries, providing an inspiration to the women of today as well as a story of life as an early missionary's wife.

[1] **First White Woman Over the Rockies**, by Clifford Merrill Drury, 1963
[2] **Mary Richardson Walker: Her life**, by Ruth Karr McKee, 1945

By the mid-1800s, the population on the Western Frontier outgrew the supply of schoolteachers, and soon the male-dominated profession was infiltrated by females. At first the schoolmarms were frowned upon because it was believed women were incapable of managing a classroom. This, however, proved to be a misconception. As thousands of schoolmarms came west with the settlers, the male population found, to their surprise, that women were quite capable of handling almost any situation, including a classroom.

When these dauntless ladies arrived, they picked up their petticoats and waded right in. Their classes were large and many of the students were rowdy, but with the no-nonsense manner and firm hand of a seasoned schoolmarm, they helped to educate the west as well as tame it.

In 1861, Hannah Clapp, an outspoken, well-educated lady from New York, traveled west to Carson City and organized the first private school in Nevada. Miss Clapp was a match for anyone doubting the ability and zeal of a schoolteacher. She was a tall, angular woman who wore dark, mannish suits with a heavy gold watch chain suspended across her ample stomach. Her shoes were flat-heeled and sensible, and her hats plain.

Miss Clapp's assistant, Miss Babcock, was a dainty, slender woman with a gentle voice and soft ringlets. She remained in the background quietly maintaining the household and helping with the classes. This freed Hannah to go about her business of crusading for anything she felt worthwhile. Often, her loud voice could be heard booming out at the town hall meetings as she fought for a cause.

This unlikely pair taught kindergarten through 12th grade for 25 years. During that time, Miss Clapp became one of Carson City's leading citizens. She was prominent in many organizations and a politically active suffragette before it became a popular issue. Many of Nevada's leading statesmen were graduates of Hannah's Sierra Seminary.

In 1887, Miss Clapp moved to Reno, Nevada, with Miss Babcock, to teach at the State University. When Miss Babcock passed away in 1899, Hannah was devastated and donated $500 toward the Babcock Memorial Kindergarten. Two years later, Miss Clapp resigned from the university and retired to Palo Alto, California, where she died in 1908 at the age of 84. She has always been remembered as one of Nevada's leading educators.

During the 1800s, teachers like Hannah Clapp and Miss Babcock were the exception rather than the rule. Few women of that era had the opportunity to attend college and express their opinions, even fewer were in a position to organize a school.

While Hannah Clapp was running her seminary and crusading in Nevada, Abigail Scott Duniway, also a schoolmarm, became one of the West's more famous suffragists. Although she had less than a sixth-grade education, Abigail became a noted journalist and dedicated leader for women's rights. She fought a 42-year battle to achieve her goal, becoming the first woman in Oregon to register to vote in a national election.

When Abigail was born in 1834, on a humble farm in Tazewell County, Illinois, her mother wept, for another daughter "was almost too grievous to be borne." At an early age, the frail little girl learned the true meaning of the word work. No matter how hard the task or how small the child, everyone in the family performed the never-ending chores. The hard work of Abigail's youth contributed to painful rheumatoid arthritis in her later years.

Obtaining an education was not easy for the child. Her first lessons were taught by her grandmother as they read Webster's Spelling Book. Abigail's school days were interrupted by chores and illness, but she continued to learn; her hungry mind absorbed everything she read.

When her father moved the family West, Abigail kept a daily journal in which she recorded the terrible ordeal of the trip to Oregon, and deaths of her ill mother and baby brother. Abigail couldn't understand how a man could impose his will upon an unwilling wife, for her mother had begged to remain behind.

Following her arrival in Oregon, Abigail became a teacher in a tiny log cabin school. Because she had only a sixth-grade education, she had to study to keep up with her students. When the Donation Land Act became law, Abigail, who had many suitors, married Benjamin Duniway, and they claimed their free acres of land for a farm. At that time, she was sure she would never suffer from overwork like her mother. Unfortunately, her life followed the same pattern of too many children and hard work, with little reward. Abigail, however, was not one to give up. In 1859, she published a novel and later wrote a column for The Farmer's Wife that exposed the drudgery of being a farmer's wife. It was at this time in her life Abigail became interested in politics.

Her husband, Ben, did not provide an adequate living for his family, and Abigail decided to turn their small house into a school with a dormitory for boarding students. She rose at 3:00 a.m. to take care of her own household chores and cooking, then taught classes all day. When Ben was injured and became a semi-invalid, Abigail sold the little school and opened a larger one in Albany, Oregon. The following year, Abigail found she was expecting her fifth child. She realized there was no way she could handle a school and a new baby, so with only $30 in her purse, the intrepid Mrs. Duniway borrowed enough money for a millinery shop and became a successful businesswoman. Working with women increased Abigail's desire to help the suffrage movement.

As soon as she was able, Abigail threw herself into the battle for women's rights. She moved her family to Portland and started printing *The New Northwest*, a weekly newspaper for women. She joined forces with suffragette Susan B. Anthony and started lecturing throughout the United States. Her eloquence and dramatic appeal were successful, and in 1883 the suffrage bill passed in Washington, but lost in Oregon the following year.

Abigail kept working. She tried again in 1900 and 1906, but lost by a narrow margin. In 1908, when the bill was again defeated, she was 74-years-old and spent most of her time in a wheelchair. Her treasury was empty, but Abigail's spirit was as strong as ever. She had always said when she went to heaven, she wanted to go as a free woman, and she did. All of Abigail's work paid off in 1912, when she proudly went to the polls to cast her vote in a national election.

When this grand old wife, mother, schoolteacher and suffragette was asked for a word of advice, she said: "Do not yield to difficulties, but rise above discouragements."

Jeannette Rankin began her career as a schoolmarm in rural Montana. Like Abigail Duniway, she was destined to move beyond the schoolroom. While the majority of women were still struggling for suffrage, Jeannette was elected to a seat in the United States House of Representatives, four years before the 19th amendment was ratified. In 1917, this free-thinking daughter of the West carried the banner of peace to Washington, D.C. in time to voice her opposition to World War One.

Although she was one of 56 representatives to vote against the war, Jeannette, because she was a woman, was singled out and crucified by the press. With rare courage that put her colleagues to shame, the lady from Montana went on to fulfill her duties as a representative and earned the respect of her constituents. In 1941, Miss Rankin returned to congress as a dove of peace, where she cast a lone vote against World War Two.

This dynamic woman was born in 1880 on a large ranch six miles out of Missoula, in the wild, gun-toting Montana Territory. Her father, a respected businessman and rancher, provided an above average income for his wife and children. There were six daughters and one son, Wellington, in the Rankin Family. Jeannette, the eldest child, was expected to assume many of the duties of caring for her younger siblings as her mother was overburdened with the household chores.

At an early age, the young girl learned to change a diaper, cook a meal and use the old treadle sewing machine. When her younger brother Wellington arrived, she favored him with extra attention, which he returned, and a strong bond soon developed between them that lasted a lifetime. In later years, he was Jeannette's constant supporter and backed his sister in all of her ventures.

When Jeannette wasn't helping her mother, she was her father's closest companion. He encouraged her to mingle with his workers and taught her how to handle his business. The girl had a rare maturity he admired. She seldom became ruffled and early in life she had the ability to solve most problems and make quick decisions. With her father to guide her, Jeannette developed into a strong, self-sufficient woman.

In the 1900s, the Rankin family acquired a large second home in Missoula. It was the envy of the neighborhood. The magnificent house, however, was not completely furnished for many years. It was a home where education and the enrichment of travel were more important than frills and fancy decorations. The children were sent to the finer schools in the east and grew into well-rounded adults who were comfortable with people from all walks of life

At 17, Jeannette was a lovely, outspoken young woman who enjoyed parties and dancing. She had a slender build, expressive gray eyes and an abundance of lustrous hair which she pulled back from her face. Jeannette's popularity and outgoing personality made her a desirable woman who received many proposals of marriage; however, she turned them down. She had already helped raise one family, and at that time in her life, Jeannette no longer wanted the responsibility of children. She was confused over her future, but eager to begin a career.

Since she had been a leader most of her life, it was natural for the young woman to lean toward the field of education. Jeannette entered the University of Montana in 1902 and graduated at the age of 22. At that time, her brother Wellington was attending Harvard Law School. In order to remain close to her home, Jeannette accepted a teaching position in a rural school. She was not quite ready to cut the bonds of her family and fly alone.

School, however, was not a challenge for the high-spirited Jeannette and soon she became restless. Her active mind needed more and it was time to move on. Wellington invited her to join him and Jeannette traveled east, unaware that the move would change her life and goals. As she had grown up in the fresh air and wide-open spaces of Montana, the poverty and squalor of the inner cities were a shock. When she observed the wretched tenements and the people struggling for survival, Jeannette knew she must do all she could to help improve their lives.

Jeannette began her battle for equality, and soon realized that unless women had the vote, they could not change society. At the age of 30, she joined the National Women's Peace Association and began to work for suffrage. When a Montana legislator announced he planned to introduce a bill for women's rights, Jeannette held him to his promise and went to Helena to speak before the House. This was the beginning of her illustrious career.

Wellington, who had established a successful law practice, decided to accompany his sister to the capitol. He knew she would need all the support she could get. They entered the House Chambers together, and when Jeannette rose to speak before the packed assembly, she was greeted by thunderous applause. Her absolute charm and total femininity dispelled the idea that all suffragettes were middle-aged and masculine. The bill, however, missed by a narrow margin, and Jeannette was determined to achieve the vote for the women of Montana.

She swept across the territory like a whirlwind. Jeannette excelled at campaigning and leadership. Her well-organized followers worked by Jeannette's side, distributing literature, visiting the small farms throughout the countryside and speaking on street corners, something that was considered unladylike and raised a lot of eyebrows. The women were dedicated and strong, and no one could stand up to Miss Rankin and her ardent supporters. In 1914, they were granted suffrage. Although they had the vote, Jeannette knew they had to gain the power to use it, so she set her sails for a seat in congress.

With Wellington as her campaign manager, Jeannette announced her candidacy in Butte, Montana. She knew this would be the battle of her life, but Jeannette was a seasoned campaigner and ready for a fight. On November 7, 1916, she won! At the age of 36, Jeannette Rankin sat in the United States Congress and she was faced with the most difficult decision in her life. The woman had grown up in the turbulent Montana Territory listening to tales of violence and the vigilantes. She wanted people to live in peace without lawlessness. Now, as a new congresswoman, she had to vote for or against America entering World War One.

When Miss Rankin appeared on April 2, 1917, at a special session, she was greeted by applause. Later, when the Speaker of the House requested the vote, she passed on the first call. As the second call came, the congresswoman from Montana slowly rose to her feet and with composure said: "I love my country and I cannot vote for war. I vote no." The newspapers reported that the lone lady wept as she cast the vote heard around the world. This was not true, there were no tears, just sadness.

Jeannette finished her term with dignity and continued to work for suffrage. The amendment was ratified in 1920 and all women were given the right to vote. During the next 16 years, Jeannette worked for women's and children's issues and the Women's Peace Movement. In 1940, with Wellington by her side, she filed for the United States Congress. Her message was: "Prepare to the limit for defense; keep our men out of Europe." In November, she defeated her Democratic opponent and returned to congress.

When Pearl Harbor was attacked by the Japanese, Jeannette Rankin was once again faced with the specter of war. This time, she drove through the streets alone seeking the right answer. Wellington had advised her to vote yes, but at 3:00 a.m. on December 11, 1941, Jeannette cast a no vote saying: "As a woman, I cannot go to war and I refuse to send anyone else." When she called Wellington, he said that Montana had turned against her. Jeannette completed her term as the maverick Republican.

On January 15, 1968, Jeannette staged her last protest when she marched with 5,000 women from Union Station to the U.S. Capitol with the "Jeannette Rankin Brigade." Participants included Coretta Scott King and Dagmar Wilson, founder of the Women's Strike for Peace. Jeannette and 16 others were in a delegation which met with Speaker John McCormack and Senator Mike Mansfield. At that time, Jeannette was 88 years old and still fighting.

Miss Rankin passed away five years later, two weeks before her 93rd birthday. In 1985, Jeannette Rankin joined the ranks of 93 other Americans being honored in Statutory Hall at the United States Capitol, including Montana's first entry Charles M. Russell, one of the West's noted and colorful artists. Although they appear to be an unlikely pair at first glance, both were creative individuals with an independence of thought and a great respect for their fellow citizens.

In contrast to the many schoolmarms who had a cause, Montana's first schoolteacher, Lucia Darling, was totally dedicated to her profession. In 1863, at the age of 24, this charming lady left her sheltered home in Ohio and traveled across the plains to teach on the frontier. Although her refined background did little to prepare Lucia for a life in the west, she successfully opened a log cabin school and taught class in the shadow of the gallows.

Lucia Darling was born in 1839 in Kalamazoo, Michigan. At the age of 10, she went to live in Talmage, Ohio, with Sidney Edgerton, her wealthy uncle and his family. She graduated from college while living there and at the age of 16 began her teaching career. When Edgerton was appointed Chief Justice of the Idaho Territory, Lucia traveled west with the family to Bannack, Montana, then part of the Idaho Territory.

Lucia kept a diary during the trip across the plains. She recorded their three-and-a-half month ordeal of traveling through Indian country and how it felt to take her turn on watch with a revolver by her side. She also told of the campfires, singing and the beauty of the West. Lucia always looked for the romance and adventure in the world around her and ignored anything that was unpleasant.

Bannack was a wild mining town filled with saloons, gambling halls and houses of ill repute. It was a place where murders occurred daily and "decent" women were afraid to appear on the streets. The feminine population stayed close to home sewing, visiting each other and attending an occasional dance or dinner party.

When the Edgerton family settled into their five room cabin,

Lucia began her search for a schoolroom. Dressed in a large, brown cape with a perky little bonnet, she and her uncle set out to find a vacant cabin. As they walked up and down the dusty streets of Bannack, they found, to their dismay, the only available dwellings were dirty and falling apart. So, it was decided that Lucia would open her school in the Edgerton's cabin.

Lucia wrote in her diary: "But into this town had drifted many worthwhile people who unbendingly held to their principles of right. There were few families and the parents were anxious to have their children in school."[1]   Then, with high expectations, the new schoolmarm opened her class. Her textbooks were few, the pupils were of all ages, and the little classroom stood in the shadow of the gallows.

Miss Darling cheerfully hung a colorful curtain over the window and soon the children's voices could be heard singing, lead by the sweet, soprano voice of their teacher. When Lucia heard a gun shot, she had the class sing louder. This refreshing lady taught her students until 1864, when her uncle became the first governor of Montana.

Lucia Darling returned to Ohio, and went on to serve as principal of the ladies' department of the Berea (Kentucky) College for 11 years. In 1885 she married S. W. Park, an Ohio businessman. During Lucia's happy marriage, she was always identified with all that was progressive and for the good of the city.

These dedicated schoolmarms, and others like them, provided a strong foundation for the building of the West. An old miner who noticed a change for the better when ladies arrived, wrote these words of appreciation: "So far as the improvement of society is concerned, one true, pure woman is worth a volume of sermons."

---

[1]**Vigilante Woman**, Virginia Rowe Towle, 1966

Hannah Clapp
Miss Clapp opened the first private school in Nevada.

Lucia Darling
Montana's first schoolmarm.

Jeannette Rankin

The first woman elected to a seat in the
United States House of Representatives.

Courtesy of the Arizona Historical Society of Tucson # 28917

The women's cell at the Yuma Territorial Prison
Pearl Hart is standing behind the woman playing the guitar.

Chapter 8

PETTICOAT PRISONERS

T he era of the Old West was the most colorful period of our nation's history. It was a time when notorious outlaws and brave lawmen became legendary characters whose names are more popular today than in the 1800s. By the turn-of-the-century though, the west was becoming civilized. Trains were slowly replacing the older methods of transportation and most of the desperados were either dead or in exile. The days of the stagecoach robberies were past; at least the citizens of Arizona thought so. All of that changed, however, on the afternoon of May 30, 1899 when two people stepped out onto the road with guns drawn, and commanded the driver of the Benson-Globe stage to "Halt!" And, the short career of Pearl Hart, who is known as "The Last of the Lady Road Agents" began.

When the stage came to a stop, three nervous passengers disembarked and obediently raised their hands in the air. They noticed the bandits were an odd pair. One was tall, muscular and sported a fancy moustache. The other smaller one appeared to be a woman whose figure was poorly concealed. She was wearing a rough miner's shirt and blue overalls, which were tucked into coarse boots that were obviously too large. A few dark curls escaped from beneath the dirty cowboy hat that covered her head and the hands that ransacked the passenger's pockets were small and white.

The haul was not a poor one. A drummer had $290, a heavy-set man turned over $36 and a Chinese merchant added $100. The robbers seemed content and the smaller one silently returned four dollars to each passenger for bed and food. Then they rode off into the bushes and the stage continued on its way at a fast pace. When it arrived in Globe, the driver ran in and notified the sheriff and an excited posse set out in pursuit of the dangerous renegades. The old-timers, however, seemed almost happy, for to them a robbery meant the Old West was still alive and kicking.

Meanwhile, the road agents, who were clearly novices, attempted to cover their tracks. They were unfamiliar with the territory and spent three days plunging across canyons and doubling back, only to find themselves a few miles from the scene of the crime. When the posse found them they were sound asleep on the ground. Neither one even had the chance to spend a penny of their ill-gotten gains.

The sheriff awakened the pair and asked the man his name. When he seemed hesitant to answer, the woman said, "Joe, it's Joe Boot." No one ever knew his true identity, so that was how he was booked. Boot didn't give the lawman any trouble, he turned himself over without a word, but the woman was not anxious to go to jail; she put up quite a fight and had to be subdued. The *Arizona Star* reported, "She is a wild-cat of a woman and had she not been relieved of her gun a bloody foray might have resulted." When they reached the jail, Pearl was carrying all the money.

The path that led Pearl Hart to that fateful day in May was long and hard. She was born in 1872 in Ontario, Canada, and christened Pearl by her mother; no one is sure of her last name. It can be assumed Pearl had a normal childhood, very little has been written about her early years. She entered a boarding school for young ladies at the age of 16, and while there she met a personable man named Hart. He swept the girl off of her feet with his looks and promises. A year later they eloped, much to her mother's dismay.

Hart was a semi-professional gambler, sometime bartender and full-time drinker who spent more hours nursing his hangovers than working. Pearl returned to her mother several times during her marriage, but Hart always managed to convince her to give him one more chance.

In 1893 they went to Chicago in hopes of finding steady employment at the World Columbian Exposition. Hart was confident he could get a good bartending job. He ended up instead as a barker in a shabby side show. Pearl, however, discovered the glamour of the West in the form of the tall, muscular cowboys who were part of the entertainment. It wasn't long before one of the amorous cowhands convinced the pretty lady to accompany him to Colorado. He paid her way but soon left her there to fend for herself.

Pearl's admiration for cowboys ended and she began cooking in the mining camps of the west. For the first time she began to save money and was doing well. Pearl especially liked the attention she received from the male population. One day in Phoenix, Arizona, she ran into her husband. When he noticed she looked prosperous he decided to get a bit of her money. Once more Hart talked his way back into her life with the usual promises.

This time he did settle down for a few years and held a steady job. During that interlude they had two babies. Hart again showed his lack of responsibility when he began drinking and abusing his family. Pearl knew she really had enough of her husband and sent her children to her mother, who was living in Ohio.

Without the babies and her husband, Pearl returned to the mining camps disillusioned with life. She drifted from place to place and soon began drinking heavily and using drugs. There were many men in her life, but she was not a prostitute.

In 1899 Pearl met Joe Boot in a mining camp in Arizona, and they became close friends. Whether Pearl was in love with Boot or not has never been revealed, although at the time of their arrest she claimed undying affection for the man. At other times, however, she expressed disgust for him and said he was weak and worthless.

Boot was with Pearl when she received a letter saying her mother, who she loved very much, was ill and needed money for medical expenses. She and Boot looked at their resources and since neither one had any, devised a plan to rob the stage. At least that is the reason they gave the police. Boot said he just went along with it to help the woman.

This was Pearl's first encounter with the law and her last, but it made headlines throughout the United States. Many newspaper reporters rushed to Arizona to write every detail of the "sordid" crime they could dig up, whether it was true or not. Pearl was portrayed as a fallen woman and described as a morphine fiend. Through the years writers have continued to tell of the notorious Pearl Hart who will forever be remembered as a stage robber.

Sheriff Bill Truman of Pima County said she was a tiger-cat for nerve and endurance and would have killed him if she could. In another report it was written, "She is a delicate, dark haired woman, with little about her that would suggest the ability to hold up a stage loaded with frontiersmen. She had refined features, a mouth of the true rosebud type, and clear blue eyes that would be confiding and baby-like were it not for the few lines that come only through the seamy side of life. In weight she is not over 100 pounds, in form slight and graceful."

Joe Boot, on the other hand, was described by Sheriff Truman as,"...a weak morphine-depraved specimen of mortality, without spirit and lacking intelligence and activity. It is plain the woman was the leader of the illy (sic) assorted partnership. She does not deny that such was the case, and expresses nothing but contempt for her companion."

The prisoners were first taken to Florence for preliminary hearings and held over without bond to answer to the grand jury. Pearl was transferred to the Pima County jail at Tucson because there were no accommodations for women in the Florence jail. It was said Pearl cried when they separated her from Boot.

On October 20, 1899, *The Tucson Star* wrote of Pearl's escape from the Tucson jail. The officers were quite upset over it as they had taken every precaution for her safe keeping. The newspaper wrote, "It is evident that after everything was quiet someone entered the courthouse, walked up the stairway and entered the tower room. It was the work of but a few minutes to cut a hole through the wall into Pearl's room. She held a sheet to catch the plaster that fell by her side. After the hole was cut through, she put a sheet underneath, and placing her chair upon that crawled through the hole."

It was obvious she had an accomplice because she couldn't have managed it alone. The police believed it was Ed Hogan, who was serving a drunk and disorderly sentence. He was a trustee and also turned up missing the next day. Pearl was captured in New Mexico several days later and returned to Tucson.

The plight of Pearl Hart won the hearts of many, especially women. She had no prior arrest and they felt she should not be put on trial, convicted and sentenced under a law she or her sex had no part in making. She captured their sympathy and used it to help win freedom. However, no one really knows who Pearl was; her personality changed to suit her moods. In the eyes of many she was a petite woman who couldn't possibly have committed the crime. Others saw her as a depraved, fallen woman. Even Pearl's vocabulary alternated between Western phrases, gutter slang and that of an educated woman. Later, during her confinement, she wrote poetry which showed an educational background.

On November 25, 1899, Pearl stood trial for her part in the robbery and was acquitted. The judge was furious and dismissed the jury. He immediately rearrested her, calling in a new jury. This time Pearl was charged with a lesser crime, stealing the revolver from the stage driver. She could not stand trial again for the robbery itself.

The *Arizona Sentinel* reported, "The action which will be telegraphed all over the country is, however, likely to do the reputation of Arizona a considerable amount of injury, as it will confirm many eastern people in the idea that the people of Arizona have a sneaking sympathy for crimes ... In these days of women's rights the question of sex should not be allowed to play any greater part in crime than it is supposed to do in merit and achievement."

The *L.A. Times* wrote, "On Pearl's re-arrest she was found guilty of robbery and languished in the prison. The jury that acquitted her on the first charge would set a premium on female vandalism. But there is only one jury like that in Arizona; bandits get their own due, be they male or female."

Pearl, at the age of 28, was convicted and sentenced to serve five years in the territorial prison at Yuma, Arizona; her accomplice, Joe Boot, was sentenced to 30 years. Throughout the trial Boot had maintained he did it only to help a lady in distress. Although both Boot and Pearl had a "death-do-us-part" vow, he escaped a few months later and was never heard of again. Pearl entered the prison on November 15, 1899. She was the 13th female prisoner and became number 1559.

The Yuma Territorial Prison, which was built in 1873 and stood on a bluff overlooking the Colorado River, was not a place one would choose to be incarcerated. Although it was a model prison for the era, most lawbreakers shuddered at the thought of spending time behind its massive granite walls which were five feet thick and seventeen feet tall. During the summer it was a Hell Hole where the sun's rays beating across the rocks frequently raised the temperature to 120 degrees. Many of America's worst criminals spent years behind those walls either praying for an early release or planning an escape, which was almost impossible.

One of the most dreaded places in the prison was the Dark Cell, a barren cage set within the hillside and devoid of light. Inmates who were caught fighting, using opium (the drug of the day) or refusing to work, were placed in the cell for a period of time. It was said that upon their release even the most hardened criminals became model prisoners.

In 1878, the first woman inmate, Lizzie Gallagher, who stabbed and killed her lover, was sentenced to serve one year in the prison. Her arrival created several difficult situations. There was no place to accommodate her; she couldn't eat with the men, so meals would have to be brought to wherever she was housed, and since all prisoners had to take a bath once a week under guard, who would watch over her! As if this weren't enough, all the men had to have their hair cut off, and that would be too cruel to do to a woman. Even clothing her would create a problem as all the males wore striped attire. The officers took the easiest way, they let Lizzie wear her own clothing and prayed she would get an early release. In Lizzie's case their prayers were answered, she was pardoned 42 days after her arrival by John C. Fremont, then Governor of The Arizona Territory.

During its 36 years in operation, 29 women were sentenced to serve time in the prison. The youngest was 16 year old Rosa Duran, who was a convicted robber. The oldest, Allegracio de Otero, was somewhere between 55 and 70. She was charged with selling liquor to a Pima Indian and arrested on a charge against the United States government. By the time Pearl arrived, women prisoners had become almost routine. What was new, however, was her notoriety. Although Pearl had only robbed once, she had become known as the female Black Bart of the late 1800s, and curious people stood in line to see the lady.

Following Pearl's incarceration in the prison, the *Yuma Sentinal* wrote, "Pearl Hart the famous bandit, was given quarters at the territorial Prison last Saturday morning. Pearl is a morphine fiend of the most depraved character and at present rather hard to get along with as the officers are endeavoring to induce her to dispense with the use of the deadly drug." It seemed the press would never leave the woman alone.

The next day a letter arrived at the prison from Pearl's brother-in-law that confirmed her first story of why she committed the robbery. It said, "To the Sheriff - I see by the papers that you have Miss Pearl Hart in custody in Arizona for some misdemeanor. Now, as I am her brother-in-law, I am interested in her welfare. It has been a long time since we have heard from her, and we did not know what had become of her. I assure you that her mother would be glad to have her at home. I have seen her sit and cry when we were talking about Pearl and wondering what had become of her....Now, I would beg of you to be as easy as you can, for we have not dared to let her mother know that we have heard anything of her and much less that she is a prisoner, as she is troubled with heart disease and the news might affect her seriously...James T. Taylor"

The letter awakened the sympathy of citizens everywhere who were following Pearl's trial. The fact that her mother really was ill and that she came from a good home made them realize that she was not entirely lost. They felt that a few years in jail would help rid Pearl of what they called her "evil passions" and become "honorable" so she could return to her mother.

Pearl was to be the only female prisoner for almost nine months. *The Arizona Graphic*, on January 27, 1900, described her quarters, "Pearl occupies a cell as large as an ordinary bedroom, which is excavated in the hill side, and she has a 'houseyard' in which to take her constitutional whenever she is minded. She is evidently living on the fat of the prison as there was a pound of butter on the table in her cell...Several weeks of prison life had relieved (her) physical system of its load of opium...She is talkative and delights to tell the story of her stage robbery."

Pearl did enjoy the many people who visited her cell. She granted interviews to those interested. Many of the visitors left feeling so sorry for her that they donated coins so she could have a little money when she was released. Pearl also began writing poetry and plays. She enjoyed reading magazines and did whatever she could to keep active. The guards often talked to her, but they didn't remain longer than a few minutes for fear of creating a scandal.

One day Pearl was so lonely she requested someone to ask the Assistant Superintendent, Ira Smith, if she could have one of the pups of Judie, the prison dog. Mr. Smith, however, declined, saying, "Judie is a lady and her pups are well bred, and I don't want to have their morals contaminated by association with Pearl." So, there was no pup in the lonely lady's yard. A few weeks later, when a visitor heard that Pearl had been refused the pup, he brought her a kitten to keep her company.

When Elena Estrada, the 14th woman prisoner arrived on October 20, 1900, Pearl was no longer lonely. Elena was a murderer and also notorious. It was said she had cut the heart out of her lover and slammed it in his face. Since he didn't die until the next day that was obviously not the case. It was merely the newspapers attempting to create a sensational story. Elena was sentenced to seven years. She was a large woman, five feet ten inches tall, who could read and write. Her first comment to Pearl was, "Did they make you cut your hair off like that?" Pearl laughed because she liked her mannish bob and definitely preferred wearing men's clothing, which looked good on her small frame.

Elena and Pearl shared the cell a little over a year, until Alfrida Mercer arrived on November 10, 1901. Alfrida had been arrested for adultery and sentenced to six months. She was a quiet little 37 year old woman. Alfrida was a temperate person and not an opium user; she was easy to get along with. The officers and prison guards felt sorry for the woman and treated her kindly.

A few days later, Rosa Duran was brought in. She was a convicted robber who was sentenced to three years, and only 16 years old. Rosa and Elena did not get along. They both had hot tempers and ended up spending three days in the dreaded dark cell for fighting.

There were four women sharing one cell, and that could be a problem. Usually Pearl was the first to complain, but when the fourth inmate arrived the others spoke up. The warden didn't want any trouble from the female prisoners, so he added another cell. This proved to be a blessing when 19 year old Jesus Chacon was brought in. She appeared to be a real tough woman as there were scars all over her body. Jesus' crime was arson; they put her in with Rosa because that would mean the two younger women would share the same cell. It would also end the constant fighting between Rosa and Elena.

The prison officials were attempting to get paroles for some of the women, citing over-crowding as the reason. They weren't the only ones seeking a release. Pearl knew she could never escape so her sister and mother, who had found out where her daughter was, were petitioning the governor for a parole. They said if Pearl obtained a release she would have the opportunity to play a leading role on the Orpheum Circuit. Her sister had written a play which would dramatize Pearl's experience as a stage robber.

The petition was convincing and Governor Alexander O. Brodie agreed to sign it if Pearl would leave Arizona. She accepted the terms and was released a little over two years from the day she entered the prison. Rosa Duran was also pardoned, and the prison officials gave a sigh of relief because that meant there were only three females to cope with.

It was said Pearl left the prison in good health and free from opium addiction. One final letter was written about Pearl on January 4, 1904. It was from the Prison Secretary, J. H. McClintock. In it he said he had escorted her to the train and that she was living with her mother. Her record while she was incarcerated was excellent, and she had devoted a lot of her time making lace and fancy work which sold well among the visitors. He further said she had consistently told him she had held up the stage solely for the purpose of returning to her home. In his opinion, her modest appearance suggested she wouldn't have the "sand" to hold up a stage. McClintock described Pearl as being polite and timid around other people during her time at Yuma.

No one knows if Pearl's stage appearance was successful. Some say she returned to drug use and became a prostitute. The end of her life appears to be as confusing and as much a mystery as the lady herself. However, that may no longer be the case. An envelope that has been marked "not for public use" has recently been opened. It's contents reveal that Pearl Hart did return to Arizona and married a well-known politician. They were married many years. During that time Pearl had one son. At the time of her death she was survived by the son, a grandson and several great grandchildren.

Although the dates are a little off, that is probably due to the poor record keeping of the 1800s, as the story appears to be true. There were also other reliable letters stating that Pearl did return to Arizona. Old pioneers who knew her, recorded their information for future use. They claimed she lived in Gila County and was "soft-spoken, kind, and good in all respects."

There is no guarantee that any of the documents are true, but they appear to be authentic. The last married name of the late Pearl Hart has deliberately been omitted from this chapter to protect her descendants. It would be a relief to write the final page in the life of the woman known as the last of the lady road agents — perhaps then she would be able to sleep in peace.

Although Pearl Hart was the most famous female prisoner, it must be remembered there were 28 other women who spent time in what was referred to as "The Hotel on the Hill." A few of them were notorious but the majority served their sentence and disappeared.

The territorial prison was as much a deterrent to crime as the bullets of the lawmen. During the 1800s, when the west was young, the vast open spaces provided favorable conditions for both individual bandits as well as gangs of desperados. There was little law outside of the six-shooter and it was said that barely one quarter of the men who were buried died of natural causes.

Since the resources were few, most of the prisons were built by the prisoners themselves. It kept them busy, provided exercise and left very little time to plan escapes. Often a dining room would serve as a chapel, laundry facility and a place to hold weekly bazaars where the inmates could have visitors and sell handmade objects.

During the 33 years the Yuma Territorial Prison was in operation there were only 29 women inmates compared to 3,000 men, making it almost entirely a male society. Under the circumstances the prison officials did all they could to provide humane conditions for both sexes. The mere fact that a woman was imprisoned proved a double hardship upon her. She was not only rejected by society but also had to live alone, completely cut off from others because of her sex.

The prisons had few facilities to rehabilitate the inmates. Those who were hardened criminals when they arrived usually remained that way. Upon their release most returned to the same life they had temporarily left behind. One of the female prisoners, Georgie Clifford, also known as Georgie Redmond, repeatedly asked for help overcoming her addiction to drugs. The system, however, did little because there was a lack of funds and they were not there to help drug users — regarded at that time with contempt rather than pity.

Georgie arrived in Arizona at the age of 17 with her husband. By the time she was 20, the young woman had a three year old girl and was addicted to opium. Her husband did all he could then took their child and left the state. Soon after, she was arrested and convicted of administering an overdose of morphine to a man, Peter Perry. After serving one year of a three and a half year sentence, new evidence was found that left a reasonable doubt of her guilt. Georgie was pardoned on February 22, 1895.

In 1897 Georgie was again in jail for cutting Henry Rubenstein, a man she was living with, with a knife. The press described her as a "pitiful object." They also said she was a "woman of powerful physique" who had knocked four men down during her arrest.

The court found Georgie insane and committed her to an asylum as a victim of both morphine and cocaine. The press again provided a description of the poor woman when they wrote, "She was an emaciated physical wreck with the skin drawn tightly over the bones of her face and hair merely a dirty yellow patch." Georgie begged the authorities to send her back to the penitentiary rather than the asylum. She knew it would not help her and said she hated the "crazy" women who would be afraid of her. It appeared she had already been admitted to the asylum once and had simply walked off.

No one knew what to do with Georgie and the woman herself declared they should just let her go. But there was no alternative, she was returned to the asylum. Georgie had fallen to the lowest depths and considered persona non grata; there was no way to help her.

While Georgie was at the asylum, Henry Rubenstein, the man she had attacked with a knife, was arrested for keeping a disorderly house. When he was questioned, Rubenstein had a lot to say about Georgie. Although he had a wife and seven children, he said, "the highest ambition of his life came to be to break Georgie of the dope habit." To achieve that he had tried to make her sick of what he described as the "stuff" and gave her all she wanted, hoping she would get her fill of it. What he did was futile, however, as she became worse and he ended up a penniless alcoholic. She had cost him $1,000 within a year.

On May 26, 1897, Georgie ran away from the asylum and had to be brought back; she was discharged one month later — it seemed no one wanted to be bothered with Georgie. Five months later she was taken from her lodging in a hopeless condition to the Florence Crittenton Home, where it was said she died of morphine and cocaine poisoning. No more had been written about the pathetic woman who was denied the help she so desperately sought — she was about 24 years old at the time of her death...

In 1901, Alfrida Mercer was convicted of what was considered a most disgraceful act, adultery. The Arizona Sentinel wrote, "It is indeed a sad case, one which calls for sympathy for the disgraced and dishonored children and father." She was the 15th female prisoner and one who the courts claimed did unlawfully, willfully and feloniously have carnal knowledge of the body of one, Frederick Croseley, he not being the husband of her.

Alfrida pled not guilty to the all male jury but was convicted on the word of Mrs. Belle Croseley (or Crosby) the wife of Alfrida's alleged lover and four others who testified against her. She was sentenced to the penitentiary for six months. The prison officials felt there were more important criminals to spend their time on. They were sorry for the poor lady and treated her kindly. Although her husband stood by Alfrida throughout the trial and promised to be there when she was released, there is no proof that the man kept his word. Alfrida quietly served her time and created no disturbances for anyone.

On February 27, 1902, Walter Trimble and his wife Bertha were arrested in La Cananea, Mexico, for the most shocking crime to hit the territory in the early 1900s; that of assault upon the alleged daughter of his wife, a child 12 years old. Mrs Trimble was accused of participating in the crime by using force against the girl, which led many to believe she was not the girl's mother. The press reported it was of such a revolting nature that the details could not be given to the public.

Several weeks after the terrible event was committed the couple decided to leave the country and were apprehended in Mexico. The girl, whose name was Lydia, was placed in the custody of Constable Hill. While she was in his care, the Constable reported the child suffered fits of insanity and during that time would tell the story of the crime. Hill said she lived in mortal dread of her step-father and at first would not trust either him or his wife.

The press reported Walter and Mrs. Trimble were a "dejected woe-be-gone" couple. Bertha was visibly affected and claimed her innocence. It was thought by many that the couple were lucky to be in custody and not the focus of a lynching party as it was such a heinous crime.

The entire community was so shocked that people crowded into the courthouse to see the repulsive defendants. Although Bertha Trimble had a veteran lawyer, she was still found guilty of the charge. Both Walter and Bertha were called fiends and were sentenced to life in prison. Since the woman reputedly assisted the man in his "vile" act, the jury felt she should also suffer the same penalty.

After serving one year, a new trial was secured through the efforts of Mrs. Trimble's sister who lived in California. Bertha's attorney immediately applied for a change of venue to move the case to another county. Not wishing to incur further expense, the District Attorney moved for a dismissal of Bertha Trimble. The offense of accessory to the crime of rape was unknown to the Arizona statutes so it was really a nameless crime.

Bertha was liberated and warned to leave the community; she

left on the first train. A few months later it was said her sister attempted to abduct, Lydia, who by then was safely in the care of a woman in California. The plan was discovered and upon questioning, the woman said she meant no harm to the child, all she wanted was for Lydia to tell the truth.

With the Trimble case again in the limelight, officials began to review the circumstances of the crime. Walter Trimble had appealed once but was turned down. During the careful investigation new evidence was discovered. When the girl testified, she had said her mother held her down and that she had attempted to fight her stepfather and that he bit her arm. The arm had been displayed in court as evidence. The new investigation turned up an interesting fact, the scar was really the result of a smallpox vaccination. Further inquiries proved the girl was subject to seizures and often lied.

Whether a crime was really committed will never be known but Walter Trimble was freed four years after he entered the penitentiary; it was said at the time he cried when his release was granted. No one knows if he rejoined his wife Bertha, or moved on alone. No further mention has been made of the child.

It has been over 85 years since the Territorial Prison was closed. As the hot desert winds blow across the old yards and rattle the iron doors, one can almost hear the voices of the past. The command post sits empty, looking down upon the vacant grounds where dangerous men once planned an escape while the women quietly watched from their lonely cells.

Today as thousands of visitors enter this historical site, now a State Park, they see pieces of history that have been carefully preserved through the years. Perhaps an old uniform, a photo on the wall of the museum, or a piece of lace that one of the female prisoners made, will catch their eye. For all, the visit is a step back in time and for one brief moment the Old Wild West lives again — most agree it is a experience that will not be forgotten.

The author would like to thank Linda Offeney, Park Ranger and Curator, and the staff of the Yuma Territorial Prison State Park for making this chapter possible. The stories of the women inmates have been taken from old documents, prison records and newspaper articles from 1878 to 1909.

Pearl Hart

*At times Pearl appeared so modest that many
people felt she was a victim not a criminal.*

Courtesy of the Arizona Historical Society of Tucson, # 28916

Pearl Hart

Arizona's lady road agent

Courtesy of the Yuma Territorial Prison State Historic Park

Pearl Hart

Mug shots

TERRITORIAL PRISON AT YUMA, A.T.

Description of Convict

Name: Pearl Hart
Crime: Robbery
Alias:
County: Pinal
Legitimate Occupation: None
Habits: Intemperate
Opium: Morphine
Complexion - Med. dark
Size of Head:
Height - 5', 3"
Color of Eyes: Gray
Married: Yes
Nearest Relative (Mother)
Can Read: Yes

Number: 1559
Sentence: 5 years from Nov. 17, 1899
Nativity: Canada
Age: 28
Tabacco: Yes
Religion: Catholic
Size of Foot: 2 1/2
Weight - 100#
Color of Hair: Black
Children: 2
Can Write: Yes
Former Imprisonment:

Where Educated: United States (Private)
When and How Discharged: Dec. 15, 1902, Paroled by Gov. Brodie
Relative - Mrs. James Taylor Jr., 712 Jefferson St., Toledo, Ohio

PRISON RECORD

The Yuma Territorial Prison Circa 1890

Georgie Clifford #947
Manslaughter 1894-1895
Georgie Clifford, age 20
native of South Carolina, was
sentenced to serve three and
one half years in the Territo-
rial Prison. She was given an
unconditional pardon by the
governor in 1895. Her addic-
tion for drugs was not under
control and she was in and
out of jail and the asylum for
the rest of her short life.

Courtesy of the Yuma Territorial Prison State Historic Park

Alfrida Mercer # 1816
Adultery 1901-1902
Alfrida Mercer, age 37 native
of Pennsylvania, was con-
victed of adultery and sen-
tenced to serve six months in
the Territorial Prison. She
was released April, 1902,
after serving the entire
sentence.

Courtesy of the Yuma Territorial Prison State Historic Park

Bertha Trimble # 1919

Rape 1902-1903
Bertha Trimble, age 37
native of Texas, was sen-
tenced to life in the Territo-
rial Prison. She was dis-
charged in 1903 by order of
the Supreme Court.

Courtesy of the Yuma Territorial Prison State Historic Park

Kate Nelson # 2219

Adultery 1904-1906
Kate Nelson, age 37 a native
of Ireland, was convicted of
adultery and sentenced to
serve two years in the Terri-
torial Prison. She was
released July, 1906, after
serving the entire sentence.

Courtesy of the Yuma Territorial Prison State Historic Park

Exie Sedgemore # 1326
Assault with Deadly Weapon
1896-1897
Exie Sedgemore, age 25 a native of California, was convicted and sentenced to serve three years in the Territorial Prison. She was unconditionally pardoned December, 1897, two months after her incarceration. There were so many letters written on her behalf that the Governor almost had to pardon Exie.

Courtesy of The Yuma Territorial Prison State Historic Park

Elena Estrada # 1685
Manslaughter 1900-1902
Elena Estrada, age 25 native of Mexico, was convicted of manslaughter and sentenced to serve seven years in the Territorial Prison. She was paroled November, 1904, after serving two years. Elena shared a cell with Pearl Hart and in 1902 she was put in the Dark Cell five days for fighting.

Courtesy of The Yuma Territorial Prison State Historic Park

BIBLIOGRAPHY

Primary Sources

Chapter 1. Horse Trading Women and Cattle Queens
Books: Burton, Mary Taylor, *A Bride on the Old Chisholm Trail,* 1939; Curry, Herbert, *Sun Rising in the West: The Saga of Henry Clay and Elizabeth Smith,* 1979; Fox, Virginia, *A Queen Named King: Henrietta of the King Ranch,* 1991; Haley, Everett J., *Charles Goodnight: Cowman and Plainsman,* 1984; Roach, Joyce Gibson, *The Cowgirls,* 1990. Special Articles: Humbolt National Forest Papers; Daughters of the Republic of Texas Library. Magazines: *Frontier Times,* Nov.-Dec., 1928, Sally Skull, Colonel Henry Perkins; IBID, Feb.,-Mar., 1966, The enigma of Juana Mestena, Dee Woods; *Southern Historical Quarterly,* Vol. 50, Jan., 1947, Lizzie E. Johnson: A Texas Cattle Queen, Emily Jones Shelton. Newspapers: *Idaho Statesman,* Apr. 1928 through Dec., 18, 1972; *San Antonio Express,* Feb., 1934.

Chapter 2. Rodeo Trail
Books: Gilchriest, Gail, *Cowgirl Companion,* 1993; Riske, Milt, *Those Magnificent Cowgirls: A History of the Rodeo Cowgirls,* 1983; Mc Ginnis, Vera, *Rodeo Road,* 1974; Ward, Betty Penson, *Idaho Women in History,* 1991. Special Journals: SideSaddle, National Cowgirl Hall of Fame. Magazines: *Real West,* Mar., 1969, Lucile (sic) Muhall, Fabulous Cowgirl; *Real World,* Sept., 1969, Cowgirls—Sugar and Spice, Louise Cheney; *True West,* Sept.,-Oct., 1967, *The Cowgirl Prospector,* Harriet Farnsworth; IBID Sept.-Oct., 1969, Lorena Trickey-Rodeo Bonanza Queen, Sam Henderson; *Western Horsewoman,* Jan., 1969, The Sage of Vera Mac, William Klutte; *World of Rodeo,* Sept., 1979, Trickey's Career Laced with Trouble, Reba Perry Blakely. Newspapers: *Cheyenne State Leader,* Aug. 11, 1917; *The Cowgirl Prospector,* Harriet Farnsworth.

Chapter 3. A Little Diversion
Books: Allen, Robert, *Vaudeville and Film,* 1980; Elliot, Eugene, *A History of Vaudeville,* 1991; Farnsworth, Marjorie, *The Ziegfeld Follies,* 1956; Furman, Evelyn Livingston, *The Tabor Opera House: A Captivating History,* 1984; Seagraves, Anne, *Women of the Sierra,* 1990; IBID *Women Who Charmed the West,* 1992; Sobel, Bernard, *A Pictorial History of Vaudeville,* 1961; Magazines: *Ladies Home Journal,* Mar.-Apr., 1926, The One I Knew Least. Maude Adams; *Sunset,* Vol 13, 1904, The Lessons of Maude Adams' Success. Newspapers: *Gold Hill News,* 1864, San Francisco Call, 1894; *San Francisco Chronicle,* 1902; *The Queen, The Lady's Newspaper* (Great Briton), 1892.

Chapter 4. Trail of the North Wind
Books: Shipman, Nell, *The Silent Screen and my Talking Heart,* 1988; Simpson, Claude and Catherine, *North of the Narrows,* 1981. Special Sources: The Idaho Film Collection, Hemingway Western Studies Center, Boise State Universtiy; Bonner County Historical Society Museum; Priest Lake Historical Society. Newspapers: *Priest River Idaho,* July 5, 1923; IBID Feb. 16, 1923; *Spokesman Review,* Feb. 22, 1987.

Chapter 5. The Horseman was a Lady

Books: Adams, Mildretta, *History of Silver City: The Story of the Owyhees,* 1960; Curtis, Mabel Row, *The Coachman was a Lady,* 1968; Seagraves, Anne, *Women of the Sierra,* 1990; Ward, Betty Penson, *Idaho Women in History,* 1991. Magazines: *Air California* Apr., 1976, Charles Parkhurst was a Woman, Anita Weier; *Bay View,* July, 1986, The Tale of Charley Parkhurst, Betty Lewis; *Farmer's Almanac,* 1974, The Story with a Surprise Ending, H.N. Ferguson; *Frontier Times,* June-July, 1971, Little Jo, Roger Rickert. Newspapers: *American Journal-Examiner,* 1904; *Golden Transcript* Jan. 14, 1885, both first and second edition; *Idaho Statesman* Jan. 12, 1904; *New York Post,* Dec. 21, 1926.

Chapter 6. Those Wells Fargo Women

Books: Bebe, Lucius M. and Clegg, Charles M., *U.S. West, Saga of Wells Fargo,* 1949; Loomis, Noel M., *Wells Fargo,* 1968; Seagraves, Anne, *Women of the Sierra,* 1990. Special Sources: Columbia State Park, California, The William Daegener Papers; Sierra City Historical Society & Betsy Cammack, Marie Devine Story; Wells Fargo Archives, *The Girl Who Drove Stage,* Lynn C. Denny, 1937. Magazines: *Californians,* Vol 11, No 3, A Turn-of-the-Century Sister's Act, William Strobridge; *California Quarterly,* June, 1970, Wells Fargo, Staging Over the Sierra, Jackson W. Turrentine; *Wells Fargo Bank,* Wells Fargo Since 1852.

Chapter 7. Schoolmarms With a Cause

Books: Bowden, Angie, *Early Schoolmarms of Washington Territory,* 1935; Butruille, Susan G., *Women's Voices from the Western Frontier,* 1995; Drury, Clifford M., *First White Woman over the Rockies*, 1963; Fargo, Lucile, *Spokane Story,* 1950; McKee Ruth Karr, *Mary Richardson Walker: Her Life,* 1945; Richey, Elinor, *Eminent Women,* 1975; Seagraves, Anne, *Women of the Sierra,* 1990; IBID *High Spirited Women of the West,* 1992; Towle, Virginia Rowe, *Vigilante Woman,* 1966. Special Sources: Excerpts from Eliza Laffayette Bristow; U.S. House of Representatives, The Jeannette Rankin Papers, 1985. Newspapers: *San Francisco Chronicle,* 1901 through 1905; *Warren Daily Tribune* (Ohio) Aug. 18, 1905, The Passing of Lucia Darling Park.

Chapter 8. Petticoat Prisoners

Books: Aikman, Duncan, *Calamity Jane and other Wildcats,* 1927; *Prisoners in Petticoats,* Elizabeth Klungness, 1993. Special Sources: Records, documents, newspaper articles and photos from the Yuma Territorial Prison State Historic Park; The Arizona Historical Society and the Arizona Pioneers' Historical Society. Magazines: Wild West, Aug., 1995, Yuma Prison, Beverly S. Markiewicz. Newspapers: Dating from 1878 through 1909: *Arizona Bulletin; Arizona Daily Citizen; Arizona Graphic; Arizona Republic; Arizona Star; Arizona Sentinel; Yuma Sentinel.*

Books

Aikman, Duncan, *Calamity Jane and other Wildcats,* 1927

Adams, Mildretta, *History of Silver City: The Story of the Owyhees,* 1960

Allen, Robert, *Vaudeville and Films,* 1980

Brown, Dee, *Gentle Tamers,* 1953

Butruille, Susan B., *Women's Voices from the Western Frontier,* 1995

Bebe, Lucius M. and Clegg, Charles M., *U.S. West, The Saga of Wells Fargo,* 1949

Bowden, Angie, *Early Schoolmarms of the Washington Territory,* 1935

Bunton, Mary Taylor, *A Bride on the Old Chisholm Trail,* 1939

Curry, Hubert, *Sun Rising on the West: The Saga of Henry Clay and Elizabeth Smith,* 1979

Curtis, Mabel Row, *The Coachman was a Lady,* 1968

Drury, Clifford, *First White Woman over the Rockies,* 1963

Elliot, Eugene, *A History of Vaudeville,* 1941

Fox, Virginia, *A Queen Named King: Henrietta of the King Ranch,* 1984

Farnsworth, Marjorie, *The Ziegfeld Follies,* 1956

Furman, Evelyn F. Livingston, *The Tabor Opera House: A Captivating History,* 1984

Fargo, Lucile F., *Spokane Story,* 1950

Guerin, Elsa Jane, *An Autobiography,* Pub. 1968

Gilchriest Gail, *Cowgirl Companion,* 1993

Holmes, Kenneth, *Covered Wagon Women,* 1988

Haley, Evetts, *Charles Goodnight; Cowman and Plainsman,* 1984

Horan, James, *Desperate Women,* 1952

Jordan, Teresa, *Cowgirls,* 1982

Klungness, Elizabeth, *Prisoners in Petticoats,* 1993

Loomis, Noel M., *Wells Fargo,* 1968

McGinnis, Vera, *Rodeo Road,* 1974

McKee, Ruth Karr, *Mary Richardson Walker: Her Life,* 1945

Riske, Milt, *Those Magnificent Cowgirls: A History of Rodeo Cowgirls,* 1983

Roach, Joyce Gibson, *The Cowgirls,* 1990

Ross, Nancy Wilson, *Westward the Women,* 1991

Richey, Elinor, *Eminent Women,* 1975

Sprague, William, *Women of the West,* 1940

Stephens, Autumn, *Wild Women,* 1992

Shipman, Nell, *The Silent Screen and my Talking Heart,* 1988

Simpson, Claude and Catherine, *North of the Narrows,* 1981

Seagraves, Anne, *Women of the Sierra,* 1990

Seagraves, Anne, *High-Spirited Women of the West,* 1992

Seagraves, Anne, *Women Who Charmed the West,* 1991

Smith, Harry, *Virgin Land,* 1950

Sobel, Bernard, *A Pictorial History of Vaudeville,* 1961

True Life Books, *The Miners,* 1976

Towle, Virginia Row, *Vigilante Woman,* 1966

Traywick, Ben T., *Legendary Characters of Southeast Arizona,* 1992

Ward, Betty Penson, *Idaho Women in History,* 1991

Wells, Kathy and Artho, Virginia, *Cowgirl Legends,* 1995

Journals

Indian Depravations in Texas, J. W. Wilbarger, 1889
The Little Lady of Triangle Bar, Frank Alkire, 1942
West Texas Historical Collection, Abilene, TS, Vol XV, Mrs. Elizabeth (Aunt Hank) Smith
Golden Transcript, Jan. 14, 1885, Mountain Charley, George West
American Journal-Examiner, 1904, Cowboy Jo was a Woman
Bay View, July 1, 1986, The Strange Tale of Charley Parkhurst, Betsy Lewis
"Idaho Film Collection" Hemingway Western Studies, Boise State University
Humboldt National Forest Papers
The William Daegener Papers, Columbia State Park
The Girl Who Drove Stage, Lynn C. Denny, 1937, Wells Fargo Archives
Excerpts from Eliza Lafayette Bristow, Oregon Historical Society
The Jeannette Rankin Papers, 1983, The United States House of Representatives

---

Magazines

Air California, April, 1976, Charlie Parkhurst was a Lady, Anita Weier
Californians, The, Vol 11, No 3, *A Turn-of-the-Century Sister's Act: Mariposa's Wells Fargo Ladies,* William Strobridge
Farmer's Almanac, 1974, Story With a Surprise Ending, H.N. Furguson
Frontier Times, Nov.-Dec., 1928, Sally Skull, Colonel Henry Perkins
Frontier Times, Mar.-Apr., 1966, The Enigma of Juana Mesteña, Dee Wood
Frontier Times, Jan.-Feb., 1971 Little Jo, Roger Rickert
Literary Digest, 1925, Mabel Strickland
Ranchman, The, Feb, 1942, The Original Cowgirl, Mildred Mulhil
Real West, Mar., 1969, Lucile (sic) Muhall, fabulous Cowgirl, Louise Cheney
Real World, May 1969, Cowgirls—Sugar and Spice, Louise Cheney
Scenic Idaho, 1952, Vol 7, The Saga of Jolly Della Pringle, Maude C. Huston
SideSaddle, The National Cowgirl Hall of Fame, 1994
Southern Quarterly, Vol 50, Jan., 1947, Lizzie E. Johnson: A Cattle Queen of Texas, Emily Jones Shelton
True West July-Aug., 1964, The Golden Queen, Harvey St. John
True West, Sept.-Oct., 1967, The Cowgirl Prospector, Harriet Farnsworth
True West, Sept.-Oct., 1969, Lorena Trickey—Rodeo Bonanza Queen, Sam Henderson
True West, July-Aug., 1983 The Woman is Charles Parkhurst
Wild West, Aug., 1995, Yuma Prison, Beverly S. Markiewicz
Western Horseman, Jan., 1969, The Saga of Vera Mac, William Klutte
World of Rodeo and Western Heritage, Sept., 1979, Trickey's Career Laced with Trouble, Reba Perry Blakely

Newspapers

Alta California, July 14, 1861

American Journal-Examiner, 1904

Arizona Newspapers: 1878 - 1909: *Bulletin; Daily Citizen; Graphics; Republican; Sentinel; Yuma Sentinel*

Austin American Statesman, Apr. 25, 1926

Corpus Christi Caller, Mar. 4, 1937

Denver Rocky Mountain News, Mar. 13, 1906

Denver Times, Sept. 8, 1901

Frontier Times, Oct., 1971

Gold Hill News, 1864

Idaho Daily Statesman, Jan. 23, 1932 & July 23, 1932

Idaho Statesman: Feb. 11, 1934; Sept. 9, 1916; Sept. 10, 1936; Dec. 18, 1936; Dec. 18, 1972

Los Angeles Examiner, Sept. 22, 1916 & July 16, 1924

Mountain Messenger, Feb. 7, 1903

New York Post, Dec. 21, 1952

Northern Idaho News: Aug. 16, 1923; May 3, 1925

Priest River Times: Feb. 16, 1923; Feb. 19, 1923; July 5, 1923

San Francisco Call, Oct. 10, 1987

San Francisco Chronicle, Nov. 3, 1894 & Dec. 2, 1902

Spokesman Review, Feb. 22, 1987

Warren Daily Tribune (Ohio) Aug. 18, 1905